The Net-Works

The
Internet

A beginner's guide
in easy-to-read
non-technical language

Scott Western

NET-WORKS

PO BOX 200
Harrogate
HG1 2YR
England

www.net-works.co.uk
Email: sales@net-works.co.uk
Fax: +44 (0) 1423 526035

Net.Works is an imprint of Take That Ltd

ISSN: 1-873668-89-0

Text Copyright © 2000 Take That Ltd
Design & Layout Copyright © 2000 Take That Ltd

10 9 8 7 6 5 4 3 2 1

Trademarks:
Trademarked names are used throughout this book. Rather than place a trademark symbol in every occurance of a trademark name, the names are being used only in an editorial fashion for the benefit of the trademark owner, with no intention to infringe the trademark.

Printed and bound in The United Kingdom.

Disclaimer:
The information in this publication is distributed on an "as is" basis, without warranty. While very effort has been made to ensure that this book is free from errors or omissions, neither the author, the publisher, or their respective employees and agents, shall have any liability to any person or entity with respect to any liability, loss or damage caused or alleged to have been caused directly or indirectly by advice or instructions contained in this book or by the computer hardware or software products described herein. **Readers are urged to seek prior expert advice before making decisions, or refraining from making decisions, based on information or advice contained in this book.**

TTL books are available at special quantity discounts to use as premiums and sales promotions. For more information, please contact the Director of Special Sales at the above address or contact your local bookshop.

Contents

Change of Address

When you try to access some of the sites recommended in this book you may come across the dreaded "file not found" screen or a similar message indicating the site is no longer located at the given address.

This isn't because we have given you the wrong address or mistyped it (though that may have happened, because we are only human!) but because the Internet is in a constant stage of flux. Every day pages are being created, but also others disappear. Perhaps a company or person has a page on a certain ISP's computer, but they found a cheaper way to access the Internet and changed ISP. So they have to take their page with them and load ed it onto another computer.

However there are a few tricks that you can try to locate the information you are after (assuming you have already checked that you've typed the address exactly as given):

■ Try changing the file name extension from *.htm to *.html and visa versa.

■ Add or subtract the "www" at the beginning of the page address.

■ Play around with the capitalisation of the address, but remember that host names are not case sensitive.

✳ ■ Remove the last part of the file name so that you are just left with the host name. You can then follow links on the site to try and find the page that you require.

If all else fails take a few key words from the page you are trying to find and go to a search engine. Even if this still does not find the site that you require you will at least find similar sites and perhaps still get the information you are after.

Chapter 1

Introduction

The World Wide Web (WWW, or Web for short) has virtually taken over The Internet. Indeed, for many people it is The Internet. Such is its rate of growth, you would struggle to believe that only a few years ago even the most informed of experts were saying that the Web would not survive to the end of the Millennium. Little did they know it would expand at such a rate that even the most computer-illiterate of people would be sucked into its hype.

Originally, the Internet, and the WWW, was an altruistic environment. It was made up mostly of academics and military types who created a community where information was readily available. Everything was free of charge and no one would have dreamed about trying to sell a product or their services. The only restriction you were likely to come across was a denial of access if

The Internet

The Internet may be dominated by the World Wide Web, but don't forget:

- **Email** - an obvious oversight, used for sending and receiving messages.
- **Usenet** - often called Newsgroups, which are communities of people with similar interests in a certain subject. Messages are posted on an electronic notice board for everyone to read.
- **FTP** - File Transfer Protocol, a method used to upload or download files from a server.
- **Telnet** - Another communications method predominantly used by a webmaster.
- **Gopher** - A menu driven interface considered to be the predecessor of the WWW.
- **IRC** - Internet Relay Chat used for live conversations.

you didn't have a password for sensitive information. But when the Net, and in particular the Web, became popular all of that changed. With so many 'ordinary' people starting to surf the Web as a pastime, it did not take long for Big Business to see it as a new way of selling around the globe. Simply by putting their products onto a computer they found that they could induce customers to shop at their leisure and buy their products in the comfort of their own home. It also captured the imagination of educators as a way of getting quite detailed information across to a large audience.

Before joining the Internet you may have wondered what all the fuss was about when you heard the word 'browser'. But it was the introduction of these browsers, used to navigate the World Wide Web, which took away the cold, dry collection of commands that computers need to speak to one another. So instead of having to type long commands and make a choice from plain text menus, browsers let you use your mouse to click away in a Graphical User Interface environment (or GUI, that's geek-speak for pretty pictures). You could say that it is the arrival of browsers that opened up the Internet to everyone.

mouse click ① By simply lifting one finger (and pressing it down again) you can receive information on virtually any subject you can think about. *no tech knowledge* ② And to access this information you require virtually no technical understanding of how you are receiving it or where it is coming *when you want to* ③ from. What is more, you can access it when YOU want. There's no viewing schedules for the Web. And, for the most part, there's *no licence fee* ④ no licence fee. What a bargain!

Life on the Web

Tescos etc Would you say you look forward to your weekly shopping - getting into the car after a hard day at work, driving through the rain and then doing battle with millions of other shoppers desperately trying to find the one product that you require hidden away in the darkest corner of the supermarket, and then standing for six years at the Express Check-out only to find you left your wallet or purse at home?

Well that is a thing of the past. Now you can order your groceries on the World Wide Web and have them delivered directly to your door! It's easy. You view the items on your computer in the same way as you would wander up and down the aisles in a real shop - but without the noise and bustle of other shoppers getting in your way. Then you make your selection by clicking on the product to put it in your shopping cart (Sorry, we'd call it a shopping trolley, but Americans invented the Internet and write most of the programs, so we are stuck with their terminology). At any point you can check what you have in your cart and you always have the option of deleting or removing an item. What is more, you will see the running total of the goods that you've selected, so staying within your budget is easier. When did you last keep track of your bill as you walked round a terrestrial supermarket?

When you've finished, you simply click on 'go to check-out'. At this point you simply enter your name and address information, tell them your credit card details and click the 'submit' button. Now a lot of people will have thought, "What? Wait a minute here. I've got to type my credit card details into a computer and send them out onto the Internet. Is that safe?" Well, at one time it wasn't. But these days most shopping sites use encryption techniques that make it virtually impossible for anyone to crack. Your credit card details are probably safer being transmitted across the Net in this way than if you were to place an order over the telephone where someone could listen in, or when ordering a product in a shop where the carbon paper of your credit card slip is simply thrown in the bin!

Anyway, let's get back to the shopping. If you are after a particular book but fed up with going around bookshops and being confronted with massive piles of the latest over-hyped cookbook, then your problems could be solved. Visit one of the many bookshops on the World Wide Web and type in the title, or even one word of the title and you will find details of the book within seconds. And, just as with your groceries, you will be able to order on-line and have them delivered to your door.

And it does not stop there. You can order virtually any type of goods that you like from CD's to television sets, and from underwear to lottery machines. You can read newspapers (containing only the news items you are interested in) and even watch the broadcasts on-line.

You can gamble all your money away or tour around one of the hundreds of museums and galleries. You can try out the latest

DOWNLOAD SOFTWARE

software and download it straight on to your computer. Then you can contact support staff or pick up the latest patch to make it work better.

BANKING

On-line banking via the Internet is with us already. If you want to find out your current balance, transfer money between accounts, pay a few bills or raise a loan you can do it all using your computer on a connection to the Web. No more queuing whilst somebody pays in £600 worth of 5p pieces they have been collecting for the last 32 years, or while a financial illiterate tries to come to terms with their latest statement. No more paperwork, and no more degrading looks from the clerks.

DOCTORS

Feeling a bit under the weather? Then why not visit a doctor. Don't go looking for the car keys, just log onto the Web. More and more doctor's surgeries are creating an Internet presence and offer diagnosis and helpful information via the World Wide Web, and it won't be long before this virtual doctor will send you a prescription straight back to your printer. Better still, they may email you a prescription, which you then forward on to a pharmacy with a Web presence who could deliver the pills through your letter box!

RESTAURANTS

Once you are cured you can go out and live it up. But first check out the restaurants in your area by consulting one of the many search engines on the Net. Take a look at their menus and book a table before you even pick up your car keys. Then nip over to a

FILM REVIEW

site which reviews films or plays to take in before your meal. If you

ORDER PIZZA

can't face going out, why not order a pizza and download the latest

DOWNLOAD MP3s

musical hits in MP3 format?

TRAVEL AGENTS

If your travels are further afield, then you can forget going down the high street to visit the travel agent. Browse the travel company's brochures at your leisure on-line and find that dream holiday you have always been looking for. And visit one or two

AIRLINES

airlines and decide on some flights that will suit you rather than the package company. Then finally book the tickets direct or visit one of the many travel agents who offer their facilities on the Net. If your wallet or purse strings are a bit tight, you'll find many a bargain on the Web. Airlines and travel companies are finding the Internet an ideal avenue for selling off their empty seats and hotel rooms at basement prices. Click tonight and travel tomorrow.

WORK DONE

Do you need a gardener, a plumber, or a builder to knock up a quick conservatory? *Then you know where to look.*

Chapter 2

Set to Surf

Surfing the World Wide Web these days really is simplicity itself. In the early days (that's about three years ago) setting up your computer system and, more to the point, loading the software necessary to join the Internet was a nightmare. The relevant browsers (software used to 'see' pages on the WWW) were created for a few systems, such as UNIX mainframes. So versions created for use on personal computers weren't well supported and crashed regularly. The worst part was getting different software programs to 'talk' to one another on your computer and then communicate everything to your modem. This was hugely ironic, considering the Internet was created so all computers could 'talk' to one another in the same language wherever they are (see Appendix B).

The Internet being the beast that it is, everything has progressed at frightening speed. In just a couple of years, manufacturers have started communicating with one another, benchmarks have been created and standard formats agreed. Well, almost. So now, most software packages are compatible. Load a new browser and it will almost certainly work with your dialer software. Add an FTP program (used for transferring files) and it will slot in beside the browser and dialer. Unfortunately you may still get conflicts, especially if you delete the files provided by one ISP (see below) in favour of another. But you are unlikely to completely wreck your system and most situations will be recoverable. Enough of the chat. This is what you need to start surfing:

WHAT YOU NEED TO SURF!
① *Computer*

The most obvious item required for access to the Internet is, of course, a computer. Make sure that it is 'up to speed'. Whilst "old faithful" may do an adequate job for you on day-to-day word processing, it may be totally useless when it comes to the Net.

The WWW is all about cool imagery (static and moving), video clips and sounds used to entertain and transmit useful information - so speed is a crucial factor. Old faithful may output one or two letters a day but could it cope with downloading a large graphics file from a flashy, new, multimedia rich site?

In essence you are going to need a computer that has been built in the last two years. Probably with a Pentium III chip, at least 32 Meg of RAM and a suitable hard disk of over 5000 Meg (Five Gigabytes). This last item is necessary to store the software you will be using to connect to your ISP plus any information, pictures or programs that you will download from the Web. Remember you'll find tons of useful, and useless, software and images that you'll want copies of - so you'll need somewhere to put it all!

A non-essential, but entertaining accessory is a sound card. Many sites now incorporate sounds into their pages, so you hear music or commentary as you move around. There are also a growing number of sites that offer radio, news and sporting broadcasts over the Net. Then, last but not least, there is the latest music technology known as MP3, which enables you to download and listen to CD quality tracks from the Web. You'll also need a soundboard and speakers to go with the sound card.

If you do not already have a computer or are looking to upgrade to a new machine from your existing computer expect to pay £800 - £1,000 for a reasonably speedy, up-to-date machine with the necessary accessories. Anything less may look a bargain but could prove a hindrance later on as modems improve, bandwidth expands and more sites go for a full multimedia approach.

② *Modem*

Notwithstanding the above, the single most important piece of equipment for your connection to the Internet is your Modem. A slow computer will still be quick enough to deal with information it receives swifter than your modem can accept it. (Remember this when you are experiencing a slow day on the Net - which happens every now and then - it is unlikely to be your computer at fault.)

A modem is a device that lets your computer "talk" down a telephone line to another computer. At the other end of the telephone line will be another modem that accepts your call and connects you to another computer which is permanently connected to 'The Internet'. Once 'joined' together, your computer becomes another part of the Net.

A modem can come in one of two forms. It can either be a card which is inserted into your computer. You then simply connect your telephone line into the back of your computer when you want to use it. Or it can be a stand-alone modem, which will either sit on your desktop or on the floor underneath your computer. And that is basically all it does. It translates your computer's data into audio tones, called modulation, and then converts audio tones back into electronic data, called demodulation. *Note: You can impress your friends, should you wish, by noticing that the word modem is made up from the first letters of modulation and demodulation!*

Since all modems essentially do the same job, the only way of discerning between them is in terms of transfer speed. In other words how quickly can they translate your data into audio tones, and audio tones back into data.

That speed is measured in terms of baud (bits of information per second). Only a few years ago 300 baud was considered the norm but today anything less than 33,600 would be considered too slow. Indeed a 14400 BPS (14.4Kbps) modem will only be acceptable if you switch off the graphics when viewing sites. But since the graphical content of the WWW makes it what it is, switching off the 'pictures' rather defeats the object of surfing it in the first place!

If you are serious about surfing you have got to look at a 33.6Kbps speed modem at least, and preferably a 56Kbps. This will give you a good speed of access to other people's sites and also allow you to upload your own pages as and when you are ready to make your own contribution to the Web.

You should be able to get hold of a 33.6 Kbps modem for around £50 and a 56Kbps external modem for around £80 - £100.

ISP

Of course it is no use having a high-speed modem if your access provider has a slower modem at their end of the telephone line.

But you needn't worry about this since virtually all access providers have at least a 56Kbps modem access. However it is still worth making a note to check that your Internet access provider does indeed have a high-speed modem connection, before signing up.

PHONE
CHARGE

Another reason for using a faster device is to keep your phone bill down. You will be 'on the phone' for the duration of your surfing session, incurring phone company charges. So the quicker you can transfer and download your data, the less time you will be on-line, and the lower your costs will be at the end of the day.

You should also make sure that the modem you are intending to buy is BT approved. While this is a requirement for all modems to be connected to the telephone line, occasional foreign, non-BT-approved modems do slip into the country, and these should not be connected to the telephone network. Look on the back of the modem for a sticker of approval to make sure.

You may also wish to buy a fax modem. These modems allow you to send faxes to and from your computer as well as creating normal links onto the Internet. Of course, it is irrelevant as far as Internet usage goes, but it is still a sensible investment and helps you further down the way towards a paperless existence.

Ensure that the modem you are about to buy comes with all the necessary cables for connecting to your computer and the telephone line. And look for offers of free software.

Installing a modem is virtually painless if you are running Windows 98, Windows Millennium, Windows NT or using a Mac. But if you are still on Windows 3.1 you could run into problems due to 'port conflict' (when two accessories try to use the same connection). Solving these problems is well beyond the scope of this publication - and beyond most people to be fair. If it happens to you, your best bet is to find someone who has already been through it themselves, buy a load of beer, and invite them round for the evening. Or, better still, bite that bullet and upgrade your operating system.

③ *Telephone Lines*

For most users a standard BT telephone line should be sufficient. Other lines do exist such as ISDN lines (Integrated Services Digital Network) but these should only be needed if you are intending to set up your own server or a high-volume Internet business. Should you decide to go the route of ISDN, check up on the different types that may be installed. There are technical reasons why some are not as good as others - although your telephone company may try to tell you otherwise. The differences are, again, beyond the scope of this publication, but now you've been alerted, you will be able to find good advice via the Web itself!

④ *Software*

The exact software that you need will depend very much on what sort of computer you have, which access provider you are using, and which services you are intending to use on the Internet.

Commercial packages are advertised and are easily available. However I would recommend that you wait and use the software that is usually provided from ISPs before splashing out. At least that way you will get to find out which functions are necessary and which are just nice add-ons. Why, for example, get all singing, all dancing, browser software that will allow you to author your own Web pages when all that you want to do is surf an hour a week?

Even once you have decided that you need some of the less common functions found on Internet software you may find that your ISP has a deal. Software manufacturers often allow access providers to offer their products direct to you at a reduced cost.

But for most people, you will find the Internet Explorer browser and Outlook (email and newsreader) software that comes with Windows more than adequate. The US justice department (and Bill Gates' competitors) may not like it, but Microsoft do produce good software!

⑤ *Internet Service Providers*

The term ISP stands for Internet Service Providers but we will tend to call them access providers in the rest of this publication since the term 'service' can mean anything in this day and age.

Finding an Access Provider

As you will realise by now an access provider or ISP is essential for your connection to the Internet and they fall roughly into two categories; those with a 'back bone' and those without.

Back bone access providers usually have dedicated, permanent high-volume connection up and down the country. They are hard wired into the Internet providing access 24 hours a day, 7 days a week, 52 weeks of the year. There isn't much that happens on the Internet without them knowing since they are an integral part of it. Generally speaking, back bone providers are more reliable than those without a back bone.

Access providers without a back bone may be able to provide you with a cheaper connection though this is not always the case. That is because they tap into somebody else's back bone and offer you a service in a different manner. What is more, non-back bone providers may not have access to the entire back bone of the access provider on which they are piggy backing.

But that all sounds like jargon. What does it really mean to you? Well, back bone providers will usually be able to offer you a better connection service than the others. By 'better connection service' we mean a service which:

- You should be able to access most of the time, instead of getting an engaged tone when you call up;

- Does not grind to a virtual standstill at busy times of the day, and

- Gives you good rates of data transfer throughout the day.

Charges

The market for Internet services is fairly intense, with the result that Freeserve finally broke the pricing mould and started to offer FREE Internet access. But, as in many walks of life, you often get what you pay for.

With the free services you will end up paying in one form or another. Some receive income by adding a penny per unit on to your phone charges. Others insist you call a premium rate line for customer and technical support. Even if you can get over these hurdles you'll find the freebies will bombard you with advertising while you are on-line. Finally, and perhaps most importantly, the popularity of these services mean they are very slow - with too many computers trying to connect at the same time. For users of these systems it

Access Provider Check List

- Is local rate or free access available?
- Is there a one-off start-up charge?
- What is the monthly/annual charge?
- What services are available?
- What speed do the ISP's modems work at?
- Do they have dedicated technical support and if so what times is it available?
- Is the technical support via a premium rate phone line?
- How much information will they allow you to store on their machine?
- Do they provide free software - is it licensed or shareware?
- Do you get free Web publishing space, and if so, how much?
- Are there restrictions on the use of that space, e.g. business?
- What bandwidth restrictions apply? If you get lots of visitors to your site, are you going to be charged?
- Is it a backbone or non-backbone provider?
- What is their connection record like?

must seem that the Internet is a very slow way of entertaining oneself.

This is particularly important if you are going to Surf at weekends and in the evenings. Most people access the WWW during these times and you may find all the lines into the free access provider's computers are in use. In which case all you'll get is an annoying engaged or line-busy signal. If in doubt, ask around and find someone who already uses the provider you are looking at and ask them if they ever experience problems. Also read one or two or the monthly Internet magazines which carry connection statistics.

Technical Support

One of the biggest factors that you should consider when deciding on an access provider is the amount of technical support they will give you. Obviously in the early days it is extremely important that you can get on the WWW and stay there with a minimum of fuss.

You will find that the quality of technical support varies quite drastically. Some access providers give you a very poor or non-existent service, whilst others are excellent and answer every phone call within seconds. Ask about the particular kind of support that is going to be available and when it will be available. If you are simply going to access the Net and use it mainly in the evenings during cheap rate it is no good having technical support that is open from 9 to 5pm.

Also watch out for the premium line services mentioned above. These seem to come hand in hand with free Internet access. You are encouraged to sign up for free, but if you then experience problems, you get fleeced at N pence per minute, where N is a big number! Be warned, even the most experienced Internet users experience some difficulty along the line.

Free Space

Sooner or later you are going to want to put something on the Web yourself - your own pages. To do this you either need a computer of your own permanently connected to the Internet, or you will need space on someone else's. Recognising this desire, most access providers now give a limited amount of free space while you are signed up with them. From their point of view it will encourage you to stay put, since changing provider will entail you moving your pages and hence changing the address. Note, however, that most providers do not allow you to use your free space for commercial activities - so it's no good if you plan selling something over the Web.

Have Modem Will Travel

As you will see there are no right ways of joining the Internet but there are plenty of wrong ways, and it is unlikely that you will get it correct first time. It is only by using the Net and gaining experience that you are going to find the right service for you. Don't worry though, because you have got a modem it is easy to swap between access providers so long as you do not get talked into a cheap, low-rate deal which is for a minimum period of a year or so. The biggest weapon you have in your armoury against being ripped off by an ISP is to increase your knowledge about the Internet.

Chapter 3

The Domain Name System

The Internet is made up of hundreds of thousands of computers all linked together for the purpose of communicating with one another. These computers may be in their own local area network which is then connected to the Internet, or they may be connected to the Internet directly. Obviously with so many computers wanting to talk to one another they need to be given names and addresses - just like humans. For example, if you wanted to send somebody a letter you first put on the envelope their name followed by their address, the town they live in and then their Postcode. And so it is with computers except they prefer to use numbers instead of letters.

These numerical addresses are stored in a collection of large databases, which individual computers then consult in order to locate the specific computer with which they wish to communicate. So the Domain Name System (DNS) is essentially like a giant map splitting the Internet into areas, cities, streets and individual houses.

Every time you go onto the World Wide Web your computer will need to use the DNS to find the pages you wish to look at. Don't worry, however, because it is not necessary for you to understand the DNS for reasons which we will come onto later. You should, however, be aware of what is going on so that you won't be totally confused when your computer produces an error message because it has failed to find the site you asked for.

IP Addresses

Every computer that is permanently linked to the Internet is given an Internet Protocol Address (or IP Address) so the other computers can find it in the DNS. These addresses consist of a

32-bit number sequence made up of four 8-bit numbers. Each of these 8-bit numbers is in the range 0-255 and the four sets are separated by full stops.

A typical IP Address may look like this:

123.255.7.193, or
140.69.4.231

Your computer will also be allocated an IP Address when you get full Internet access. If you are using a Point-to-Point Protocol connection (PPP) your host computer will allocate a new address every time you log on. Otherwise you will be using a Serial Line Internet Protocol (SLIP) connection and you will get a fixed address.

Have you got that? Good. Now you can immediately forget it all again. Because you are unlikely to ever see IP Addresses referred to like this. It is a plain fact of life that people are not as good at remembering sequences of numbers as computers are. Instead we prefer to use names and words.

Naming Domains

Alongside the numerical IP Addresses, computers (or, more accurately in most cases, disk space on computers) are also given more recognisable names in plain English, like:

net-works.co.uk

which is a lot easier for us humans to remember. You can see how this is fairly similar to the numerical IP Address in that the different sections of the "English" address are separated by full stops (usually pronounced "dot").

- The .uk part of the address tells you that the computer is in the United Kingdom;
- The .co tells you that the computer belongs to a company; and
- The net-works tells you which company's computer you are looking for.

These "English" addresses are stored along side the IP Addresses in the DNS. This is so the computers can still use the numerical sequences as their preferred way of referring to one another, and then use the English names as a way of communicating the information back to us.

So the sequence of events is something like this. You type in a Domain address such as net-works.co.uk and your computer immediately refers to the Domain Name System database via a link to the Internet. From the database it finds the 32-bit numerical address it requires and uses a standard protocol known as TCP/IP (Transmission Control Protocol/Internet Protocol) language to find and talk to the computer you requested. If you then ask for some information from the person or company at the other end they will ask you for your address which you will naturally type in English. Their computer will then use a similar process to look up your address in the DNS so their computer can talk to yours.

Interpreting Domain Names
Take the Domain previously mentioned:

net-works.co.uk

This indicated a computer, or some disk space on a computer, assigned to the company "net-works" (Usually spelt Net-Works) who are situated in the United Kingdom. (If that company had been located in France then the final two letters of the name would have been .fr) So the new Domain Name would have been:

net-works.co.fr

Similarly if it had been located in Japan the last two letters would be .jp and the address would become:

net-works.co.jp

If the company net-works is a non-profit organisation then it would have been given the letters .org instead of .co. So its Domain Address would have been:

net-works.org.uk

and if it had been part of the Government you would have the letters .gov to become:

net-works.gov.uk

These identifiers are known as Top Level Domains and those currently supported by the group which looks after these things are:

Name	Description
com/co	Commercial organisations
edu/ac	Educational institutions (universities etc.)
org	Non-profit organisations

net	Networks (usually connected via a gateway)
gov	Non-military government organisations
mil	Military government organisations
int	International organisations
uk	Two-letter (ISO) country codes, such as fr & au; uk is United Kingdom. There are more than 250 of these.

Look out for newcomers on the block, which should come into being once all the various committees can put their own self-interests aside and sort themselves out. New top-level domains on the cards include:

firm	Businesses or firms
store	Businesses selling products
web	Sites related to the WWW
arts	Sites for cultural and entertainment activities
rec	Recreation and entertainment sites
info	For sites offering information services
nom	For personal home pages

The .uk section of the domain name is referred to as the Country Code, and the .co section is the Top Level Domain. Then the "net-works" description refers to the Second-Level domain name and is usually assigned to an organisation of some sort. So, net-works.co.uk is a second-level domain of the .co and .uk Top Level Domains.

You will see a similar construction for a second level domain of your Internet service provider. The domain demon.co.uk refers to a computer in the United Kingdom belonging to an organisation called Demon Internet. In this instance however the organisation (Demon) has a large Internet presence and may have several computers connected to the Internet.

Each of these computers will be given a distinct name which is added to the front of the domain name. So a computer known as bluebird and belonging to the organisation Demon would have the domain name bluebird.demon.co.uk. There may be several of these computers each with a different name but they will all be part of one site with the domain name of demon.co.uk.

URL

URL is short for Universal Resource Locator and it allows you to specify an exact page on the Web. For example the URL:

http://www.net-works.co.uk/books/n8422.htm

consists of three main sections.

The protocol name (http://) indicates the way in which you are accessing the data. All pages accessed on the World Wide Web use the "http:" protocol name whereas a document accessed using File Transfer Protocol uses the "ftp:" protocol name. There are many other protocol names for various Internet access methods such as Gopher and Telnet which you need not worry about as they have been largely superseded.

The domain name (www.net-works.co.uk) is the name of the computer or part of the computer used by the organisation net-works (the publishers Net-Works). The www indicates that the computer contains information which can be viewed on the World Wide Web. The resource location (/books/n8422.htm) indicates the exact location of a specific page or file on the net-works computer. Just as you store information on your own computer in directories or folders so the information is stored on a World Wide Web Server Computer. So the above resource location indicates that you need to look in the sub-directory books to find a file called n8422.htm. Your Browser will then be able to open this file and you will be able to read the information contained in it on your computer screen at home.

Some URLs, you will notice, may not give an exact resource location. For example:

http://www.net-works.co.uk

In this case the Server will display a default page also referred to as the "home page" for the domain. You will sometimes see this in your browser address box. For the Net-Works site, the default is called home.htm. But, for example, the Lottery Company's default home page is called index.html

Accessing a URL

Whenever you see a URL, in a magazine, on the television or on a leaflet, you can access that information simply by typing it into your Browser and hitting the return button (see Chapter 4).

Usually you won't need to type the "http://" section of the URL since your Browser will often take this as read. So to access Net-Work's home page you type www.net-works.co.uk and press the enter key.

At this point it is worth remembering that you are dealing with computers who are an extremely pedantic species. Even if you get the URL slightly wrong you will receive an error message. Points to note here are:

- Don't leave any spaces when you type a URL. Spaces are not allowed in URL's and if you see one typed in print then it will be by accident.

- Type the URL exactly as you see it making sure that you match lower and upper case letters exactly. Most, but not all, servers won't let you access a document unless you match the capitalisation exactly.

- Look out for the extension on the resource location. Some World Wide Web documents have the extension .htm whilst others have the slightly longer version of .html - make sure you get the right one.

- Find the tilde (~) on your key board. The origin of the Internet is closely connected with UNIX computers and as a result many home directories begin with a tilde. This is not a mistake as at some point in your career you will need to type it.

The Good News

Chapter 6 will deal with navigating around the World Wide Web in more detail. However you will be pleased to hear that typing URL's is not very common. This is because the World Wide Web uses a system of hyperlinks to allow you to navigate around the system. All you need to know is how to click your mouse, with no typing involved.

Simply by clicking on a linked word, sentence or graphic your computer will be instructed to search for a specific URL linked to that word, sentence or graphic.

Chapter 4

You and Your Browser

In the beginning there was one decent browser known as "NCSA Mosaic". This was the software that revolutionised the Internet and started the upsurge in the popularity of the World Wide Web. Then half of the team that put the software together quit and started their own company. And so it was that "Netscape" was born. They produced several versions of the Internet browser software that allowed users to view pages on the WWW and it became the leading piece of software for use on the Net.

But success breeds imitation and Bill Gates and Co did not like being left behind by a group of upstarts, so they threw billions of dollars at the project and came up with their own browser called Internet Explorer. Now Microsoft have one massive advantage, apart from money, over most software manufacturers. And that is that most PCs use Windows as an operating system (the software which basically allows a computer to run). So it was simplicity itself to start including a free copy of the Internet Explorer (IE) software on the same CD as the latest upgrade to Windows. They also managed to persuade computer builders to pre-install Internet Explorer on new machines.

Pretty soon most computer users found themselves with a copy of IE on their machine. Being lazy, and not understanding much about computers, software and the technical background to these things, most of us simply used what was there. As a result, most Web surfers used IE. Web page designers then had to make their pages look good in the IE browser (pages actually look slightly different depending on which browser you are using). And, you've guessed it, because most pages were designed for IE, even more people decided to stick with it.

All of this has rather marginalized Netscape and all other browsers to the state where an average Internet user probably isn't aware that other browsers exist.

All of this is the subject of heated legal debate in the USA, which has been running for years and will continue to do so. Can you imagine the amount of money the lawyers are charging? But don't cry too much for those Netscape entrepreneurs – they made their millions by selling out to a major ISP.

With due respect to Netscape and the emerging Linux, this publication will go with the flow and concentrate on the Internet Explorer browser. If you are using something different, you will find 95% of the text just as applicable to what you see and do.

Apart from allowing you to see the pages stored on other computers around the world, which form the World Wide Web, the main function of the browser is to allow you to navigate between the different computers. The whole subject of navigation will be covered in the next chapter, so this section will concentrate on the "look and feel" of your browser along with the other buttons and menu items which do not relate to navigation.

Installing and configuring your browser is beyond this text and it is assumed that your Internet Service Provider's installation software will have installed it correctly so that it communicates with your dialer and you have no problems connecting to the Internet.

Logging on to the Internet

Connecting to the Internet with Microsoft Internet Explorer is simplicity itself. Just select >Start, Programs >Internet Explorer. Alternatively double click on the Explorer shortcut icon on your desktop. You will then see a "connect to" dialogue box which allows you to choose which ISP you are connecting to (you may use more than one service) enter your username and password.

The same box also has an option field for changing your connection setting such as the phone number that you will dial to connect to your Provider. Usually you will not need to change this but if your Service Provider has more than one connection point and the one which you wish to use is busy, you could try typing in one of their other phone numbers and connecting to a different set of modems.

Once the connection procedure has been followed your browser will display the Default Start Page that is configured within the browser. Usually this will be the home page of the Company that has provided the browser. For example, if you got Microsoft

Explorer with your computer or your Windows 95/98 CD you will probably find that your default start page is the Microsoft home page at http://home.microsoft.com/

Another possibility is that your ISP has configured the browser to display their own home page when you first connect so you can see the latest news from your Provider and see what is happening on their server.

These default start pages can be a little annoying as they leave you with a feeling of being pushed into seeing what Microsoft or your ISP will want you to see. Since every-thing you will look at will be your own personal choice, by typing in URL's or hitting hyperlinks, this procedure feels "unwanted". However the good news is that you can change this default start page to the one you prefer. This publication will show you how later.

Understanding the Screen

The illustration overleaf shows the Microsoft home page as viewed with the Microsoft Internet Explorer browser version 5.00. Since Internet Explorer is the most used browser in every country around the world the following sections will describe features and elements of the Explorer browser. We'll use version 5 as a basis, and you'll find many features are the same in older versions. Where there are major differences, we'll mention them. Users of alternative browsers will be able to follow this easily since there is very little difference in the main features of all browsers. This is hardly surprising since the various software programs are all designed to do exactly the same job.

Title Bar

This shows you the "title" of the document you are currently looking at. In the example shown overleaf the title is "Bookshop Central -

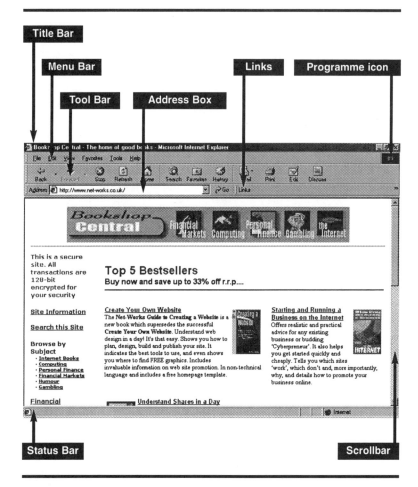

the home of good books" and is the title set by the person who created the page (called the webmaster).

Menu Bar
These are drop down menus for your browser's main commands.

Tool Bar
These are graphical buttons, which can be pressed with the click of your mouse and show the most often used commands available on the browser.

Address Box

This is where you type in the URL of a Web page that you wish to visit and if you have been using hyperlinks it will show the current Web address of the document you are looking at. Although it is called "address" in Internet Explorer you may find that it is called "location" or "net site" in other browsers. Click on the arrow at the right of the address box to see a drop down menu showing a list of pages you visit regularly.

Links

These may appear next to the address box or the toolbar depending on which options you have selected (from the View menu bar). Click on the links button to see a new set of buttons which will connect you directly to special Web pages. A default set may have been placed there by Microsoft or by your ISP. They are customisable, so feel free to delete the links you've been given and add your own. Doing so is very easy. Visit a website that you want to add to your Links toolbar, then click on the small page icon that appears on the very left of the address (looks like a sheet of paper with the letter 'e' on it). Then simply drag that onto your links bar.

Program Icon

When this icon is moving, or is "animated", the browser is downloading information from the World Wide Web. (It's an hourglass shape that keeps going upside down)

Scroll Bars

These bars will appear when a document is wider or longer than your window size. As with all other programs click the scroll arrow to move in the direction indicated. You can also drag the boxes along the scroll bar or click to the right or left (above or below) the boxes.

Status Bar

This gives you information about what your browser is doing and varies considerably between browsers. Usually it will say something like "done" if the page has been fully downloaded or "loading image 6 from 11" if it is still receiving information.

The Tool Bar

As indicated above, the main items on the Tool Bar are for navigating around the World Wide Web. There are some interesting buttons you should be aware of:

Stop

Quite simply stops your browser downloading information from the World Wide Web. This may be because it is taking too long and you are bored, or you have made a mistake in the URL that you have typed. You will also have to hit the stop button sometimes before your browser will allow you to go forwards or back in your work.

Refresh

This will get you a new copy of a document you are wishing to look at. This may sound a bit daft - what is the use in getting another copy of something you have just looked at? But you are underestimating your computer's ability to put words in your mouth!

When you type in the URL of a site that you have already visited the information that your browser needs may still be stored in the "cache" on your computer. In which case the browser will automatically load the information from the cache instead of down-loading it from the Web, which will take longer. For example, say one of your favourite sites on the World Wide Web displays a new painting every week. That painting will enter your browser as an image file with a name something like painting.gif or painting.jpg. So next time you try to connect to that Web page your computer will search for an image file called painting.gif and will find it in the cache to load it directly onto your screen. In this situation you would hit the refresh button so that the browser is forced to connect to the Web site again and will download the new painting.gif that you wish to view.

A handy hint is also to use this button when a page has taken a particularly long time to download. Try hitting the stop button and then the refresh button and quite often you will find that the page will load quicker than it was doing before.

Back

Hitting the Back button will take you to the page you have just come from. This is usually the last page you viewed. In some cases, when you are travelling a tortuous route around the Net, your browser may 'decide' that you didn't mean to go to a particular page (usually if you didn't stay there for long and went straight back to the page you were on before). In this case, it will forget that page as being insignificant and you'll find that you can't actually go back to it! More of that later...

Forward
The opposite to Back. If you have previously gone back from a page or pages, you can use this button to go Forward to it again.

Favourites
Also known as bookmarks. This is a stored list of your favourite Web sites and will be covered in more detail later in this chapter.

Print
Clicking on this button will send the current page that you are viewing to your printer.

Home
Click on this button to go to the page you have defined as the home page for the browser.

Mail
This will give you a drop down menu allowing you to start up your email and/or newsreader program.

More Things You Can Do With Your browser
One of the main drawbacks of the World Wide Web is perhaps its strongest point - its graphical richness. Sometimes, when Web usage is high, it can take a long time to download images for a page that you wish to look at. So you can speed things up by taking the option of not downloading images. In Internet Explorer click on Tools, then Options. Then click on the tab labeled Advanced. Halfway down the list you will see a section of options called Multimedia. Check or uncheck the adjacent boxes to allow your browser to download pictures, sounds and video clips. The less that it downloads, the quicker you will view pages. Once you have had a look at the page without the images you may decide that you would like to look at them so simply click on the images individually

or undo the changes you made above, then hit the Refresh button.

News and email

With IE, clicking on the Mail button initiates a drop down box. Click on the options to open Outlook or Outlook Express. These separate, but associated, programs allow you to send and receive email and to read messages in Newsgroups. These functions aren't really anything to do with the World Wide Web. They are, instead, other features that, together with the WWW and others, make up the Internet. You can read more about them in Chapter 13.

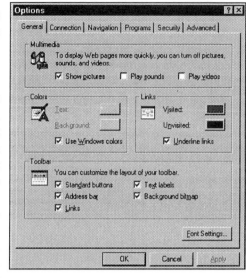

Right Mouse Button

Microsoft Internet Explorer makes use of the right button on your mouse to give you a list of the most useful commands wherever you are on the World Wide Web. Hold down the right mouse button to see what is available – these will vary according to what you are looking at and where your mouse is hovering. For example, if your mouse is over an image the options will include:

- **Save image as...:**
  allows you to save the image to your own hard disk;
- **Set as wallpaper:**
  puts the image up as the background to your desktop; and
- **Properties:**
  will tell you the name, type, size and location of the image.

If, however, you are hovering over a link the options include:
- **Open:**
  moves your browser on the new page as directed by the link;

- **Open in new window:**
  does the same but the new page is displayed as if you had
  started your browser again; and
- **Print target:**
  will send the new page to your printer

If you are not over a link, image or any special effect, you will see navigational options such as Back, Forward, Refresh and Print.

Copying Text

You can copy text from Web pages just like you would from any other document. Simply highlight the section that you wish to copy and choose "copy" from the edit menu and paste it into any text editor such as a word processor or an email program.

Saving Pages

Saving a page as a bookmark or a favourite simply puts a link in your browser so that you can go back to the page next time you are on-line. If you want to read it off-line (particularly useful if there is a lot of text) you may want to save it to disk. Go to the file menu, choose save as and you will be given the option to save the pages in html (Web) page or as text.

Selecting html allows you to view the page with your browser again going to the file menu and selecting "local file". Saving the page as a simple text file will remove all the hypertext tags so that you can read it using the word processor.

Viewing the Source

Once you have been around the World Wide Web for a while you may be interested in putting your own pages up on the Web. The good way to start this off is to look and see how other pages have been created. You do this by looking at the 'document source' which can be selected by going to the view menu and clicking on Source. You will be able to see how different Web authors use features such as 'meta tags' and 'frames' to enhance their Web sites.

Plug-ins

Plug-ins are handy little programs that work in conjunction with your browser to perform a particular function. This includes playing music, watching video clips and viewing special features on some sites such as Flash graphics. Without the plug-in you will not be able to hear or see some features on multimedia sites.

There are literally hundreds of plug-ins to perform special tricks with your browser and they are covered in more detail in the next chapter. How much you will need any of these Plug-ins is open to debate and your own preferences, but they don't do any harm and are usually small in size so they won't clog up your hard disk.

Favorites

Whenever you find a page on the World Wide Web that you think you would like to pay another visit to you can save its location by adding it to your favourites or bookmarks. Simply go to the menu bar or tool bar select 'favorites' and then click on 'add'. Alternatively, right click your mouse and select 'Add to favorites...'. Note that the software uses the American spelling of favourite, without the 'u'!

Now, every time that you are on the Web, you can go back to the favorites bookmark and simply click on the title of the page that you would like to visit. This will immediately open the page using your browser and allow you to view the latest contents. Pretty soon, however, you will find that your favorites folder may become so full of your favourite sites that it is very near useless. Just take a look at some of the favourites I have collected in the last month. They are automatically sorted into alphabetical order based on the first letter of my description. So if I click on favorites and try to find the latest price for my Shell shares (and I want to do this quickly if the markets are crashing) I would probably have to scan the list two or three times to realise where I have saved it. Not very useful. It could cost a fortune.

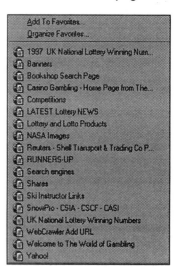

Bookmarks for the month as sorted by Internet Explorer - not easy to 'scan' with the eye very quickly

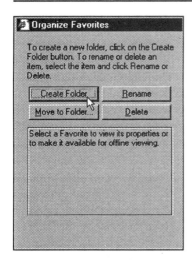

Favourite bookmarks sorted into logical folders

It would make sense therefore if I were to organise these favourites into sub folders with more accurate descriptions. And the good news is that Internet Explorer makes this is a relatively easy task.

The first thing to do is to decide how you are going to organise your favourite sites. Look at the sites you have already saved and try and think of a way of categorising them. Looking at my bookmarks you will see that these fall roughly into five different types of site; Lotteries, books, search engines, shares, skiing.

Apart from telling you something about my fragile psyche this gives an indication of useful titles of the sub menus that I should place these favourite places into. So that is exactly what I will do! Click on 'Favorites' and then 'Organise'. A new dialogue box will open with 'options' to create a folder, rename a file, move a favorite into another folder or delete a favorite. The process is very much like working with your Windows Explorer. Indeed, it is perfectly possible for you to organise your favorites using Windows Explorer.

Changing the Starting Page

The creators of your browser or your Internet Service Provider want you to go to their page on the World Wide Web in order to get some free marketing. So they will have inserted their URL in the default start page of your browser. Unless you have got some strange behavioural disorder, in which case you may want this information, it is probably better to change your start page so that it is actually useful.

Do this by going to the Menu Bar and Tools. Then click on Options followed by the General tab. You will be presented with a screen which looks like that shown. In the Home-page address box carefully type the URL where you would like to start and don't forget to leave in the "http://" part of the address. If, for example, you make heavy use of search engines you may want

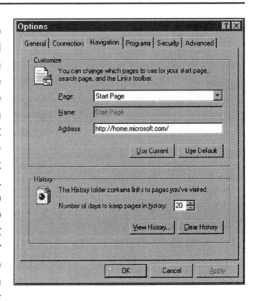

to start your browser in a search engine as a way of kicking off your surfing. So in this situation you may insert the URL: **http://www.lycos.co.uk** to start your surfing at the Lycos search engine. Close the dialogue box and you are on your way.

An Alternative is to use your browser to go to the page you would like to start at. Then follow the same instructions to open the Options dialogue box. Now this time click on 'Use Current'. The browser will insert the URL of the page you are currently viewing as your start up page. If you change your mind, go to another page and repeat the process. After a while, you may decide the manufacturers were right after all. In this case click on the 'Use Default' button. The third button, 'Use Blank' enables you to create an HTML page of your own, on your computer, which it will open when started.

Making pages available for off-line viewing

This function goes hand in hand with your favorites. When you make a Web page available off-line, you can read it when your computer is not connected to the Web – in your own time without having to worry about your phone charges or tying up your phone line. It is also useful for viewing Web pages on a laptop, say on the train, where a connection to the Web would not be feasible.

You can specify how much content you want to make available, such as just the text on a page, the page with all of its images or a page and all of its links. You can also choose how you want to update that content on your computer. You may ask the computer to automatically connect to the page every time you go on-line to check if the content has been changed, or you may specify that it checks say, once a month.

There are several ways you can save the Web page, from just saving the text, to saving all of the images and text needed to display that page as it appears on the Web.

To make the current Web page available off-line follow this procedure. On the Favorites menu, click Add to Favorites. Then, select the 'Make available off-line' check box. To specify a schedule for updating that page, and how much content to download, click Customize, then follow the 'Wizard' instructions on your screen. Note that before you go off-line (disconnect from the Web), you should make sure you have the latest version of your pages by clicking the Tools menu and then clicking Synchronize. In previous versions of Internet Explorer, off-line viewing was called 'subscribing.'

Send

The final function on the browser worth mentioning at this juncture is the 'Send' option. You obtain this by first clicking on 'File' from the Menu bar. Selecting this option gives you three further sub-options. These are to:

- **Send the current page by email.**
  This quite literally takes the html of the page you are looking at and emails it to the recipient. When they open their mail they will see the page as it should look, as opposed to just the code.
- **Send as a link.**
  This will send the basic page (no images) as an insert plus a link for the recipient to click on to see the page. This is a lot quicker as the file will be smaller.
- **Shortcut to desktop.**
  This puts a shortcut on your desktop. Click on the shortcut and it will open the browser and go straight to the page you have saved.

Web Accelerators

Once the initial euphoria and excitement of joining the Internet has worn off, and you feel like a Web expert, it won't be long before you start to get frustrated at the speed things happen. As webmasters continuously strive to make their sites bigger better and flashier than the rest, and as surfers demand evermore entertainment from the website, so the size of the files and pages increases. Also the word is out about the World Wide Web and everybody and his dog seems to be jumping on the Super Highway. The end result is that the communication lines are becoming clogged with files being transferred backwards and forwards and the whole thing often grinds very nearly to a halt. It is not uncommon, at busy times, to have to wait nearly a minute for a complex page to download. Although this isn't actually a long time it seems like an eternity when you're staring at a screen.

Web accelerators are a crude invention, which attempt to cut down on your waiting time. While you were looking at and reading a page, which you have requested in your browser, the accelerator program is working away in the background trying to guess where you're going next. By looking at your previous surfing history and noting down which sites you visit the most or from a database which you can set up within your accelerator, it will be downloading pages that you have not yet requested onto your hard disk. So when you then move on to looking at those pages they are already cached on your hard disk and load almost immediately into your browser. And when the process works in this manner it really does feel as if your browsing has been accelerated. Where you would have had to wait a minute or two to get everything you wanted it's there right in front of you within seconds.

Web accelerators work in two different ways. The first generation blindly downloaded every page linked to the one you are currently viewing. So no matter which link you click on next, the program will have cached it onto your computer and will load it immediately. When that new page is loaded the accelerator again sets about caching every page that is linked from the new one. This works fairly well unless there's a lot of links on a page then there's a good chance that the accelerator will not have fetched the link you are about to select and/or it will download a lot of irrelevant information.

The second generation only downloads links that you have visited before and if you frequently re-visit a certain set of sites this method of acceleration is much more effective for you. Accelerators have to work closely with your browser in order to function properly and this can be quite complicated. So you may find that setting up a browser accelerator is quite a difficult process. Some have to be chosen to load immediately when you start your PC otherwise they won't work with your browser, whilst others actually have to be 'installed' into the browser's software.

The Downside

So, apart from occasionally downloading pages that you don't want to see, what are the downsides of browser accelerators? Well, the fact is that they simply exacerbate the problem. Sure, the accelerator will speed up your own personal browsing speed because ·it's busy caching every page that's linked to the one you're viewing. But bear in mind your modem is requesting information from a lot of other computers and bringing it to yours for your personal use. This all takes up band width and leads to a general slowing down, albeit very small, for everyone else. Now imagine if everybody used accelerators there would be the same number of people on the Web but ten times more pages would be being downloaded at any single time. So, it follows that the Web would be responding ten times slower than if no one had accelerators. In conclusion, if you're on the World Wide Web just for your own gain and don't really care about anybody else accelerators may be a good idea. But if you are a community person and view the Internet as it was originally intended – as a place where everyone freely helps everyone else – then you will steer clear of browser accelerators.

Popular Accelerators

There are many accelerators, some are free, others you have to pay for. You'll find more details and downloads at these sites:

NetSonic	www.web3000.com
Webcelerator	www.webcelerator.com
BoostWEB	www.boostweb.net
NetAccelerator	www.imsisoft.com

Chapter 5

The World of Internet Plug-ins

The speed at which the World Wide Web has attracted non-technical users to the Internet has been nothing short of astounding. The rich mixture of images with text, and of course useful information, has captured just about everyone's imagination. But this pace of development shows no sign of abating, and the Web is becoming more dynamic every day. You are no longer faced with a static medium but with one that moves, talks and interacts with the viewer. There is still a long way to go and much of the multimedia content on the Web resembles a child taking its first steps when it learns to walk. The video may be a little jumpy, the sounds not so clear, and the interactivity may sometimes go astray, but a start has been made and everyone is beginning to see how the Web will grow up.

Your basic Web browser is designed primarily to view static websites. In order to see video footage, listen to sounds and music, or to perform any other function it requires something that's known as a plug-in. Different browsers treat these plug-ins in different manners. With Netscape Navigator the plug-in is treated as a separate entity altogether. If you come across a site that requires a specific plug-in, whilst using navigator, the browser will tell you as much and ask whether you would like to get the plug-in or ignore the feature on the site. Once you've acquired the necessary, you will more than likely have to quit Navigator and re-start it before it becomes active. Internet Explorer, on the other hand deals with plug-in technology in a very different manner. Microsoft prefers to call its browser enhancements ActiveX components. These components are designed to install themselves when you visit a page with multimedia content. This makes dealing with plug-ins much easier for Internet Explorer users than for Netscape users. In addition you will find that Internet Explorer can use some of Netscape's special plug-ins as well. However if you are adding these "alien" plug-ins you will need to install it manually from the plug-ins' folder inside the program's directory.

The plug-in software does not have a special place on your computer and they can install themselves almost anywhere. So removal is not a simple operation. If you do, for any reason, wish to remove a plug-in you will need to manually search for the files and

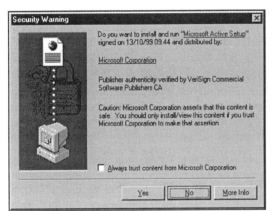

then delete them. You can do this by clicking on your start button and going up to "find files" and "folders". Perform a search for files ending with *.ocx extension. When you've found them click on the "properties dialogue" box and you will find out the name of the creator of the file which will give you a good idea of what it does. If you can then identify which plug-in you wish to remove, simply delete the file.

Here is a list of some of the more popular and useful plug-ins for both Internet Explorer and Netscape Navigator. All of them should enhance your browsing experience to some degree and since the files are fairly small there is rarely a reason to not accept a plug-in.

RealPlayer

RealPlayer has essentially become the standard for Web based video production. It's used to broadcast in real-time, streaming audio and video files of news bulletins, sports commentary, and standard radio fare.

Video picture quality tends to be fairly poor. But the advantage of Real Media files is that it plays as soon as your computer starts to receive it. In other words the computer is buffering the file and playing it while it's receiving the rest of the information – so you don't have to wait for the entire file to download before you can start to view or hear its contents. Although real video files are fairly rare on the Internet you will find plenty of audio files that make use of the RealPlayer plug-in. You'll find that you are able to down load promotional tracks from popular bands through to entire albums from those you'll have never heard off.

QuickTime

QuickTime started as a Macintosh development and, like RealPlayer, it can play various sound formats as well as films. It is used to seriously integrate video into a Web page or you can open the program as a separate window on your desktop. In other words once you have got the QuickTime files you can play them without booting up your browser. Later versions of QuickTime support Macromedia Flash and MP3 Files as well as letting you explore Interactive 3D environments.

Flash

Macromedia's Flash is perhaps the most versatile plug-in of recent years. This is because the images that it displays are saved in 'Vector' as opposed to bitmap format. So the images are re-sized by the viewer and look good in any resolution. The consequence of Web designers being able to use such a vector format means that the files you receive are smaller in size and so can be downloaded much quicker. Where Flash is integrated properly you can hardly notice any change in your browser from what looks like a static image becoming animated. You are most likely to see Flash used to create animations of text and graphics, dynamic menus and to generally boost the feel of a site through other visual enhancements.

Macromedia claim that there have been more than 150 million downloads of Flash and server logs indicate that only 1 in 10 people opt to view a non-Flash version of a Web site.

Shockwave

This was Macromedia's first attempt at Web technology and dates back to prehistoric times (that's 1995)! It started life as a way of bringing movies onto the Internet but got slightly side tracked.

You are now most likely to come across it as an alternative to JAVA on many sites where it is used to provide an interactive game such as Noughts and Crosses, Blackjack or Solitaire.

PDF

The Adobe Portable Document Format is used by Web site creators as a way of making sure that you view the page in the manner that they wish you to. You may be aware that your browser will show text and graphics in positions determined by the browser as opposed to the Web site creator. Although they can get round this factor by using tables and other tags in their page, two different browsers will display the same page in a different manner.

A PDF file will, on the other hand, always look the same. So if someone creates a magazine using Adobe PDF they can make sure that it looks the same to a surfer using the Internet Explorer browser as it does to one using Netscape Navigator.

Crescendo

This is the most popular music plug-in which is used to play back midi files. Once installed it allows you to use Internet Explorer or Netscape as a off-line midi hi-fi player so you can play music back through your computer at any time. You will find that there are thousands of midi files out there on the Internet but many of these will definitely make you question other people's taste in music.

Beatnik

Midi files are smaller than many other music files because they use the sound card to create the noise that you hear as opposed to containing the notes themselves. So if you listen to the same midi file on two sound cards you will hear a different noise from each. Now, just as many magazine publishers prefer to control what you see by using Adobe and PDF files some musicians like to control exactly what they publish in a sound file. Beatnik allows them to do this.

The file format used by Beatnik is called RMF (rich music format). This format gives the musician true control in their compositions and allows the files to be streamlined enough for easy Internet download. Some of the best examples of RMF files can be found on the MTV site and at other radio stations. Beatnik also has an interactive role. If you visit the MTV site and download some of the tracks there you can use Beatnik to re-mix them in real time. So if you've ever fancied yourself as a bit of a DJ you can set yourself to work with Beatnik without having to invest in the proper kit.

VRML

Virtual Reality Modelling Language enables the Internet Explorer browser to move around three dimensional environments. These are almost exclusively limited to role and game playing situations where you control the 'life' of an Avitar which inhabits one of these worlds. VRML does also have some non-frivolous uses for architects wanting to see what a new building or design would look like from various viewpoints and for engineers who might be wanting to see how an operator could move around a new piece of plant before it is created.

NET2Phone

This is a Netscape plug-in that allows you to use your Internet connection as if you were making a telephone call. Contrary to common belief this isn't just for making a phone call to another computer which also has the NET2Phone plug-in but it can be used to make a call to a real telephone. You will obviously need a sound card and a microphone as well as the plug-in to take full advantage of its capabilities. However, if you can put up with the relatively poor quality on the line you will be able to save a lot of money on international calls.

Sources of Plug-ins

Here are a few sites where you can obtain the latest versions of most plug-ins for Netscape and ActiveX components for Internet Explorer. Some are specifically for plug-ins and nothing else, but most carry plenty of general Internet software, which can further enhance your Web experience.

Microsoft	windowsupdate.microsoft.com
ZDNet	www.zdnet.com/swlib/internet.html
Plug-in Plaza	browserwatch.internet.com/plug-in.html
Winfiles	www.winfiles.com

Chapter 6

Navigating the WWW

There are literally tens of millions of pages of information on the World Wide Web, and each of these has its own URL. So one of the most important things that you need to know is how to get around this plethora of information. It would be folly indeed just to dive in at the deep-end every time you go surfing and just thrash about until you find some information you are interested in. So one of the first things you need to know is how you get to certain places and, if need be, get back again.

Hyperlinks

When you look at just about any page on the World Wide Web you will notice that some of the words and phrases are underlined and probably in a different colour. These are called hyperlinks or simply "links". Quite simply the creator of the page has embedded some code "underneath" these words which will allow you to go to another page on the Web which contains some more information on those words.

For example, if you came across the text: *"Faced with possible Government intervention, many on-line organisations are seeking to establish a universally accepted code of practice detailing how potentially objectionable material should be handled."*

If you were to click on the hyper-link "on-line organisations" your browser would connect to a new page on the World Wide Web most probably detailing some of the on-line organisations involved in this initiative. Also, if you click on the link "code of practice" then you would expect to progress to a page which talks about this specific code of practice, or codes of practice in general.

Of course, not all underlined words or coloured text are hyperlinks. Other ways of telling if words are linked to other pages is to move your mouse pointer over the top of the text in question and see if it changes shape. If the pointer changes into the figure of a little hand then that is a signal that you can click on the link and move to a new page. You will also notice the status bar at the bottom of your browser will display the address of the page that you would go to should you click on the link.

Links are not limited to text. The creator of the Web pages could cause almost any form of image to link you to another page. Usually these images will be in the shape of a button to make it obvious that you are connecting to another page. But it could be any form of picture, or even an area on a picture. Again, if you are not sure, try moving your mouse pointer over the top of the image and watch for it changing shape and the URL appearing on the status bar.

Also try moving your mouse pointer around any particularly large images that you see, especially those on home pages. You may find that the image contains several links pending on the part of the image that you are looking at.

Forward and Back

Let's go for an imaginary surf. Say you connect to your Internet Service Provider and you change your browser so that the default page is the Yahoo search engine. This page loads fairly quickly and you type into the main search section "cars" and hit the search button. Yahoo thinks about your request for a few tenths of a second and sends back a page of links and descriptions of pages that contain information on cars.

On this page you find some information on Mercedes Benz, a car which you have always fancied. Although you have not got enough cash you can always dream, so you click on the hyperlink and go to the home page for Mercedes Benz.

After looking down the home page you spot an image of a sporty-looking saloon and when your mouse goes over the top it goes into the shape of hand. So you click on the image and are sent to another page on the Mercedes Benz site that gives you a full description of all their passenger cars along with technical spec. At the bottom of this page are three words underlined and separated by dots. One says home, one says Team Mercedes and the other says dealerships. So you click on the latter and are sent to a page listing all the dealers in Mercedes Benz passenger cars.

Now at this point you find your dreaming is taking you a little far and you realise it is pointless even looking to see if there is a

Yahoo Search Page

↓

Search results

↓

**Mercedes Benz
Home Page**

↓

Passenger Cars

↓

List of Dealers

dealer in your area because you cannot even afford a Reliant Robin. However you would like to go back and have another look at the details on the saloons. But there isn't a link on the page of dealers that says 'passenger cars'. So what do you do?

This is where the "back" button on your browser comes in handy. It is represented by an arrow pointing from right to left and is usually situated on the left hand side of your button bar. Click your mouse over the top of this button and your browser will re-load the last page you were at, in this instance the page about passenger cars. Click on it again and you will return to the Mercedes Benz home page. Another click would take you to the Yahoo search results for "cars" and a final click would take you back to the Yahoo initial search page. At this point you are back at the beginning of your surfing session and there weren't any previous pages. So you will find that the back button on your browser will become dimmed and it won't allow you to press it.

The "forward" button works in much the same way and is

represented by an arrow going from left to right, usually the second button on your button bar. As you might have guessed pressing this button takes you to the next page in the sequence that you have been looking at.

So if you are at the Mercedes Benz home page clicking on the forward button would now take you to the page on passenger cars. A second click on the forward button would take you to the dealership page. Of course, you must have previously been to these pages for the forward button to function. Once you have arrived at the dealership page the forward button will be dim and it is no longer selectable.

That's History

Since your browser is able to take you forwards and backwards to the sites that you have been visiting you might be getting the idea that it is keeping a list - and you are right. This list is known as the "history list" and it is stored on your computer's hard disk. It is quite simply a

list of sites that you may have visit-ed on the Web during your present session or recent sessions. This is stored in the order that you visited them for the first time and provides a basis for navigation with the forwards and backwards button. Clicking the back button will take you up the list while clicking the forward button will take you down.

At each point that you stop at in the list the relevant page will load into your browser.

Once you have been surfing for a while you may decide that you would like to go back to a site that you last visited a few sessions or a couple of days ago. In this instance you can hit the back button as much as you like but you'll probably get nowhere near what you want. You can shortcut the process by going direct to the history file.

Click on the history button on your toolbar. You will be presented with a window detailing all the sites that you have visited over a

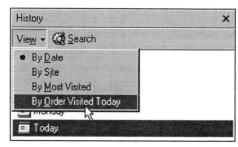

certain number of days. By right clicking on any of these and selecting 'Properties', you will then be able to see:

- The title of the page;
- Its URL or Web address;
- The date you last visited;
- When it "expires"; and
- When it was last updated.

Simply double click on any of the sites to pay another visit. This is a particularly useful function in Internet Explorer as it allows you to sort the sites you have visited by any of the above categories. Clicking on 'View' in the History window gives you the option of sorting your history file by date, by site, by the number of times you have visited them and by the order in which you visited them.

A recent addition to IE allows you to search through your history file to find that elusive site. This is, perhaps, one of the most useful functions in your browser and often overlooked by many surfers.

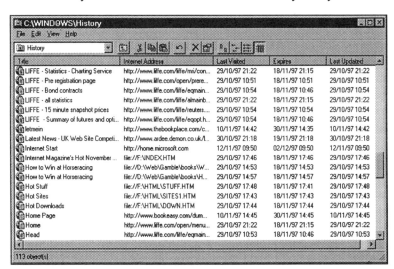

If you are a prolific surfer you will often wish to go back to a page or a site but you can't quite remember where it was that you saw it. In the old days you used to end up cursing yourself for not adding it to your Favorites list. Then you would have to go through the whole process of visiting a search engine and browsing through lots of pages again in order to find what you want.

Now you simply type a keyword into the search box and IE will do the work of looking through all the pages you have visited. If your keyword appears on the page it will be listed along with the page title. Hover your mouse over the top of the link to see the URL of the pages it is suggesting. Once the page you have been looking for has been found you can click on the 'stop' button, and then on the link to go back to the page. If the result is listed in black, the page you want should still be stored in your computer's memory. If it appears as a light blue, the computer is remembering the page's location but has removed the actual page information and graphics, so you will have to go back on-line to view it properly.

Can't Go Back

Occasionally you will come across a curious feature of the browsers. You will be looking at a page on the Web and wish to go back to one that you have recently visited. You know it was only a couple of pages ago but no matter how hard you search using the back and forward button you cannot find it.

This is not an error and your machine is not about to crash. It is actually the browser being very clever - trying to speed up your session (though some would say it is too clever). The history list is arranged so that it will ignore none productive site trips on your searching sessions.

This is best illustrated by way of example. Remember you went on an imaginary surfing session at the beginning of this chapter. Now say you made a mistake along the way and ended up at a page that you really did not want. You started with the Yahoo search page, entered the phrase "cars" and received a page of search results.

Looking down this page you spot the word Mercedes and click on the hyperlink. But instead of going to the Mercedes Benz production car home page you find that you have located some information on the Mercedes Benz racing team. You are not

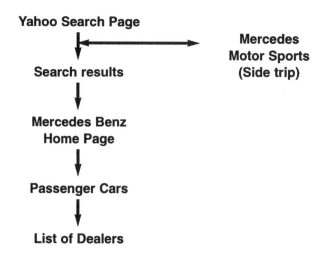

Yahoo Search Page
→ ← Mercedes Motor Sports (Side trip)
Search results
↓
Mercedes Benz Home Page
↓
Passenger Cars
↓
List of Dealers

really interested in motor racing so you hit the "back" button straight away. This takes you back to the search results page find the correct link and progress to the Mercedes Benz homepage, followed by passenger cars and then dealerships.

You will see that this imagin-ary surfing session is the same as the original apart from the little "side trip" to the motor racing page. In this instance, starting from dealerships, you will click on the "back" button to go to the passenger cars page and then to the Mercedes Benz home page. Now you would expect ano-ther click on the "back" button to take you to the racing page. But this does not happen. Another click of the button will take you back to the Yahoo search result page for cars. And when you go forwards again you will go back to the Mercedes Benz home page.

The reason for this is that your browser realised that you clicked on a link and then came straight back to the page it started from. So it assumes that you do not like the page you have been to and would never like to see it again. Most of the time this is very convenient, and the browser designers have got it right - the page you visited was not of

---

TIP

If you are browsing sensitive information and you do not want anybody else to know which pages you have been visiting, the history list can be a liability. Anybody else accessing your computer can go along to the history folder and see where you have been rather like following foot prints in the snow. If you would like to cover your tracks click on 'Tools' and then 'Internet Options', and the 'General tab'. In the history area of this screen you will notice a button marked 'Clear History'. Click on this and (some of) the evidence will be removed! Don't be lulled into a false sense of security. You will leave other footprints which those in the know can follow.

---

any use so you do not want to go there again. But there are odd occasions where you will visit a page and think "oh I will come back to that " and then exit using the "back" button. And that is the last you will ever see of it!

Site Navigation

A site on the World Wide Web is simply a collection of Web pages normally stored on the same computer and usually concerned with the same subject or company.

For example, at the Mercedes Benz site you will expect to find pages relating to their cars, servicing, accessories, dealerships and everything relating to Mercedes Benz cars. So each page deals with a certain aspect of information and together they make up the "Web Site".

Another example would be The Lottery Company site which is found at the address: **www.lottery.co.uk** offering nearly 100 pages of lottery results, news and information. All of the pages are situated at the same site and on the same computer but they have different URL's.

When a company or individual creates a Web site they try to group all the information together in a logical structure, just as they would in a "real life" shop. And to help you look around the shop they put up various signs to help you navigate your way around.

These are known as 'internal navigation aids' and consist of links that the Web authors have included in the pages to help you find your way around. These internal navigation aids are often presented as both links connected to images or buttons, and text-only versions of exactly the same links.

Why not take a look at the aforementioned Lottery Company pages by way of example? Enter the address: **www.lottery.co.uk** in the URL box of your browser and hit return. You will find a screen with the lottery company banner in the middle of the screen surrounded by small lottery balls. The balls have been labeled with titles such as 'Main Lottery Results' and 'Thunderball Results'. These titles give you a clue that the images could be linked to another page. So hover your mouse over top of one of the balls. You'll see that it changes shape into a small hand. Click on the 'Main Lottery Results' ball and your browser will connect to another page on the lottery site. This one, you've guessed it, displays the latest lottery results from the UK National Lottery main draw. If you had clicked on the 'Thunderball Results' you'd have received the Thunderball results.

If your modem had been slow or you didn't have time to wait for the small images of the balls to load, you would have noticed small boxes on the screen where the balls would later appear. An alternative text has been put into these boxes by the webmaster. This text is the same as appears on the balls, so you don't have to wait before knowing which area to click on. Finally, as another helpful navigation aid to the same pages, the webmaster has put plain text links underneath the images.

Down the left hand side are another set of links. These are to a totally different set of pages. Here you can click to find Lottery FAQ's – short for frequently asked questions, such as 'how does the Thunderball draw work?', or 'can you play the lottery from

overseas?' There's a link to an online game called Fantasy Lottery, and you can even ask the site to generate six random lottery numbers to play in the next main draw.

These links, inserted by webmasters, make moving around a particular site fairly easy and act like road signs. Once you are within a site if you were to use the back and forward buttons you will find that it is easy to become confused as to which direction you are heading in.

This is because the site is not built in linear fashion. In other words you do not enter at the home page and progress through a series of pages until you reach the end. It is more like a tree where you start at the base and move along the branches getting closer to some information but further away from others.

Finally you will notice an advertising banner across the top of the screen and two smaller banners on the left hand side panel. These are linked through to the advertiser's site. If you click on them you will leave the lottery site and surf your way through to another site.

Frames

Web designers can divide a page into two or more independently scrollable windows called frames. They are useful in that it allows a designer to put a "table of contents" in one section of the screen and allows you to view the individual pages of information in the other frame. This allows you to jump around the site more easily than is possible by only using the contents panel to make your links. However they are not very popular with some designers because it means an active search engine will not index all of the pages the site has to offer. (More of this in *Creating Your Own Website*, also published by *Net-Works*). Also browsers are not very good at remembering which frames have been visited and from where.

Try it for yourself. Find any site that uses frames and go two or three links into the site. Now try navigating around the site using the back and forward buttons. Perhaps everything will work as it should but you may find that the back button will always put you back to the home page or even throw you out of the site altogether.

Other Navigation Aids

By now you already have the basics to allow you to navigate your way around the World Wide Web. However there are a few more aids available to you. The "Home" button. This is located on your button bar and will take you back to the browser default starting page. The "Search" button.

This is also situated on the browser's button bar for Internet Explorer users. It will load a page of search services based at Microsoft Network in a side panel (where the Favorites and History Files usually appear). You may customise this page to help you search the Web quickly.

Favorites

This was discussed in the previous chapter and gives you a quick way of jumping around the sites that you find most useful.

URL box

Don't forget that clicking on the arrow to the right of the URL box will display a selection of sites from your history list.

"Go" command

Clicking on the command to "Go" from your command line will simply send you to the address in the Address panel – it is similar to hitting the return key on your keyboard.

Starting page

Perhaps one of the most useful aids to navigating around the Web is where you choose to start off.

If you wanted to spend a week exploring the Scottish Highlands you would not choose a hotel in Birmingham as your base. Each day you would have to drive all the way up the M6 to before you even got close to the places you wanted to visit. Instead it would make more sense to base yourself in Edinburgh or Glasgow.

So carefully consider what you would like as a default start page in your browser. If you look for a diverse array of information on a regular basis then a search engine makes a sensible place to start.

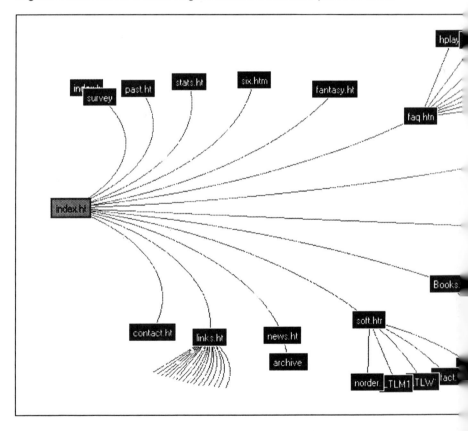

The complexity of a website makes it advisable to use internal
Continuously hitting the back and forward buttons w

If, however, you are usually interested in one particular type of information such as investment data and only occasionally look at other sites then you may wish your browser to start at a page of investment information links.

It's Not There!

There are two main reasons why your attempt to locate and retrieve a page on the World Wide Web may fail. Firstly, and most commonly, the page you are trying to get has moved or never existed. Secondly, usually when you are starting on your surfing career, you have mistyped or misunderstood the URL. Here are some of the more common errors:

File not found

If the file you are looking for has moved or changed its name then you will get this message which is known on the Web as a "404" after the error code that is produced for your browser.

Apart from the page having moved (or never existed in the first place) make sure that:

- You have matched the capital and lower cases exactly;
- You have not included spaces in the address, since these are not allowed in URL's;
- You have correctly typed any symbols such a s the tilde and underscore correctly;
- and you have got the right extension for the page e.g. html or htm?

aids whenever possible.
get you lost!

Illegal Domain Name

If you go to an illegal host name then your browser will give you this error message. The most common reason for this is that you have mistyped the address. Each of these will give you an example:

http//net-works.co.uk
http:/www.net-works.co.uk
http://www.networkscouk
http://www.net-works.uk

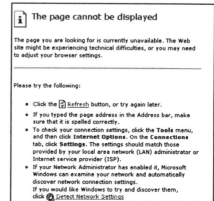

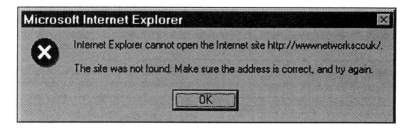

Incorrect Host Name

This is when you are trying to access an address that does not exist and has no entry in the DNS.

Host Busy

With increasing regularity, due to the number of people joining the World Wide Web, the host serving the page you are trying to access will become overloaded. This is because too many people are trying to access the page at the same time. It is usually a temporary error and it can be overcome by trying again later (in particular when the locals will be asleep - like accessing American sites during our morning).

Help Me

You will be an extremely lucky person if you do not come across one or more of these errors every week. Indeed you may come across "file not found" by trying to access some of the pages recommended in this publication. This isn't because we have given you the wrong address or mistyped it (though that may have happened, because we are only human!) but because the World Wide Web is in a constant stage of flux.

Every day pages are being created, but also others disappear. Perhaps a company or person has a page on a certain ISP's computer, but they found a cheaper way to access the World Wide Web and changed ISP. So they have to take their page with them, load it onto another computer, and get a new address.

However there are a few tricks that you can try to see if the page really does not exist or that something is slightly wrong:

- Try changing the file name extension from *.htm to *.html and visa versa.

- Add or subtract the www at the beginning of the page address.

- Play around with the capitalisation of the resource, but remember that host names are not case sensitive.

- Remove the last part of the file name so that you are just left with the host name. You can then follow links on the site to try and find the page that you require.

If all else fails take a few key words from the page you are trying to find and go to a search engine. Even if this still does not find the site that you require you will at least find similar sites and perhaps still get the information you are after.

Chapter 7

Searching the Net

It may be hard to believe these days but there was a time when only a handful of websites were available on the World Wide Web. And this was not way back in ancient history but probably no more than 10-15 years ago. In those days regular users had to memorise the addresses (URL) of the sites that they were interested in, if not all of the sites that were then available.

However, this situation did not last for long as the number of websites started to blossom. As soon as there became more than about 50-100 sites it was obviously impossible to memorise or even keep a hand written record of all the addresses available.

The obvious solution to this was to keep a personal list of sites that you knew about, on your own computer. In that manner you could keep track of all the URL's you could think of that were relevant to you, and then look at the list whenever you needed to find something. But what would happen if a new site came onto the World Wide Web and you knew nothing about it. It would not be in your list so you could not find it no matter how closely you scoured the results.

So friends and colleagues started exchanging lists and consulting one another's small databases of websites. In this manner they got a better coverage of what was available and consequently a better chance of finding the information they required.

As with all things to do with computers there were a few individuals who took things to extreme. Two of these were University students called David Filo and Gerry Yang who started to make a catalogue of as many websites as they possibly could and put them into a database. They then created a website of all these listings and wrote the code to link each individual line of the list to the site itself. And so it was in 1994 that Yahoo! was born. This became the first Web directory and set the two creators on the path to a multi-million dollar fortune.

To start with, it was fairly unsophisticated and simply listed the sites under fairly broad category headings. But the boom in the number of websites caused the pair to sit down and figure out a more clever programming technique which would allow people to use their site to find what they wanted. Before long they came across search technology that allowed users to type in words or phrases at the top of the page and make a search of the database of websites.

Modern Search Engines

With a massive increase in the number of World Wide Websites, today's search engines include an absolutely massive database at their core. These index complete lists of websites and information resources right across the Internet, and all of them aim to contain details on just about every legitimate website available. Modern search engines fall essentially into three categories:

Passive search engines

These search engines are possibly more accurately referred to as directories. They rely on World Wide Web users to submit details of their site or their favourite sites in order to build up a database. Upon receiving the submissions somebody from the search engine company trots along to the website suggested, has a look at it, and then places the details in the right part of the database by finding main category and sub-categories into which the website should fall.

Active search engines

These engines rely on search programs known as "spiders" or "Web robots" to index and categorise Web pages as well as websites. The spider travels out into the World Wide Web in search of new sites and reports the results back to the search engine. It downloads all the information that the page contains and then examines that information to extract key words and phrases that can be used to categorise the site. The exact method that it uses to do this, and which information it looks at to create the index, varies according to search engine. Those words and phrases are added to the database along side the URL and a description of the site.

Meta-search engine

This is a search engine that uses other search engines to give it the information. So when you type a word or phrase into a Meta-search engine it will consult with all the other directories and spider based search engines to gather a list of sites that you may be interested in.

Directories

The creators of Yahoo!, David Filo and Gerry Yang, may have started Yahoo! in their back bedrooms but in 1996 the company they created went public and raised over $800 million. This obviously gave them a huge amount of capital with which to improve the search engine. As a result they can now index over 1,500 pages per day into their database. Yet you may be surprised to learn that even this rate does not keep up with the speed at which new pages are being added to the World Wide Web. You will find the main Yahoo! site at: **www.yahoo.com**

With its undoubted popularity, Yahoo! has spawned area specific mirror sites. The special UK version can be found at: **www.yahoo.co.uk**

Despite its "age" this is probably still the most important of search engines available on the Web. It is easy to use and has more useful links than you can think of. Information is sorted into categories and sub-categories. There are fourteen main subject categories:

- art and humanities
- business and economy
- computers and Internet
- education
- entertainment
- government
- health
- news and media
- recreation and sports
- reference
- regional
- science
- social science
- society and culture

Each of these categories has many sub-categories and those sub-categories also contain their own sub-categories, and so on almost ad infinitum.

There are two main ways of using Yahoo! The first is to browse through the categories, and the second is to search the database.

Browsing Yahoo!

Finding information in Yahoo! through browsing s probably best illustrated by way of example. Since you have bought this publication you are obviously interested in Beginners guides to the World Wide Web. So trot along to the Yahoo! UK home page and have a look at the main categories (mentioned above).

The obvious place for starting to look for information on the World Wide Web is in the main category heading 'Computers and Internet'. Indeed, listed underneath this main heading one of the sub-headings shown on the home page is 'WWW'. Click on the hyperlink 'Computers and Internet' to find the list of sub-categories, (see screenshot 1 overleaf).

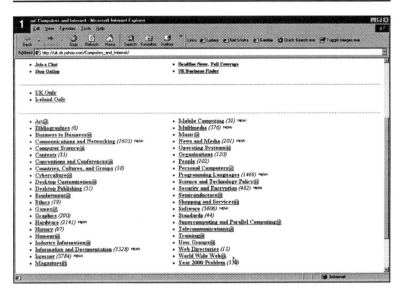

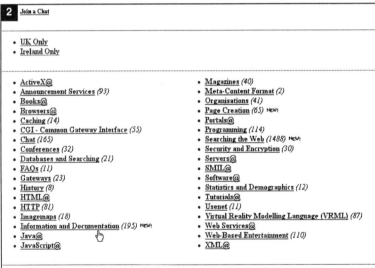

Notice the Title Bar tells you which level of category you have entered. Since the World Wide Web is our main interest here, click on the 'World Wide Web@' link.

Once into this sub-category you will find a load more sub categories all with some form of connection to the WWW. There's

3

UK Only

- Beginner's Guides *(58)* NEW
- Evaluation *(8)*
- FAQs@
- How to Search the Web@
- HTML@

- Mailing Lists *(1)*
- Page Design and Layout@
- Site Announcement and Promotion *(45)*
- Tutorials, Demos, Talks *(26)*
- Web Directories *(10)*

- Dr Keyboard 🔊 - computers and internet columnist for the Times newspaper.

- Webmaster Reference Library ꓲ꓾ꓮꓮꓲ ✦✔ - comprehensive reference for HTML authors and webmasters, the WMRL has carefully selected and annotated web sites plus original articles about the art of web site creation.

- 3D Graphics for the World Wide Web: The Basics - How to add 3-D Graphics to your Web Page.
- Atomor Web - designing web pages and getting your site listed in search engines.
- Beginners WWW Page Starter Kit - browsers, Html editors, images, forms, tables, imagemaps, transparent Gif's, templates, graphic tools, icons. download all software direct from site.
- Build a Safer Web Site - tips on lowering your legal risk when running a Web site, even when the laws are uncertain.
- CyberWeb [charm.net] ꓲꓮꓮꓲ꓾ - a major web developer resource, bridging the spectrum between W3C and Yahoo by providing local content and thousands of links to further information.
- Developer.com - information and resources for internet and intranet developers.
- DevGuru - featuring references for ASP, JavaScript, Jet SQL, style sheets, and VBScript. Also provides tutorials.
- Digitalauthors.com - provides news, reviews, tutorials, templates, design tips, and other development resources.
- Digitalrelief.com - contains tools and resources including Perl scripts, downloads, domain search, and more.

4

FAQ - World Wide Web ✦✔

- All About the World Wide Web
- Beginner's Guide To Life And The Internet - succinct and easily understood guide for Internet novices (written by a novice!).
- Beginners' Central - nline tutorial for new internet users.
- Creative Good: Help Pages
- Draac.Com - offers information on web page design, HTML, and more.
- Eric's Page - offers help with building Web pages.
- Exploring the World-Wide Web - self-directed tutorial for new web users.
- Finding a WWW Host for Your Project - Single page of suggestions on how to find a free/low-cost host for your WWW pages.
- Folksonline - for newcomers & non-technical folks. Inspirational stories, how-to articles, web tours all written by our community audience about their web experience.
- How to Publish on the Web ꓲꓮꓮꓲ꓾
- ICYouSee Guide to the World Wide Web - a project of the Ithaca College Library designed to serve as a self-guided Web training page.
- Internet 101
- Internet Brothers - offers internet helpware and tips for the cybercommunity.
- Internet Tourbus, The - presents a virtual tour of the Internet, delivered by email.
- Kitty Locker's Introduction to the Web - introduces university students to the Web, with links for research tools, designing web pages, job hunting, organisations, writers' resources, and more.
- Lepak's Home - features email etiquette, beginner's guide to HTML, web design hints, newsgroups, cv writing, and more.
- Michele Web - offers a step by step tutorial for building a website.
- Sites to See - introduction to the Web.
- SquareOne - browsing, downloading, zip/unzip, FTP, e-mail, plug-ins and more. Subscribe to the free newsletter.
- Surf University
- Tek Camp for Kids - step-by-step tour of how to use and navigate the Web.
- W3Nation - resources for beginning web developers including tutorials, tips, news, reviews, free images, and more.
- Web 101 - from Webmonkey.
- Web Site 101
- Webbery and Nettery - advice on how to go about setting up a new website - with special emphasis on what to do before writing any code.

everything from ActiveX links (which were discussed in the previous chapter) through to Security links, and from History through to Statistics. See screenshot 2. Let's not get sidetracked. We are looking for a beginner's guide so click on 'Information and Documentation' to arrive at screenshot 3.

5

Navigating the World Wide Web

"Saddle your dreams afore you ride 'em." - Mary Webb

An Overview of the World Wide Web
  If you've never seen the World Wide Web, or if you've done a bit of surfing but don't really understand what's going on, then you might appreciate this introduction page.

Finding Something On The Web
  Looking for general information on a subject? Or are you seeking a specific web site? These search and index links will help you find what you want

A Consumer's Guide to Search Engines
  Already familiar with search engines but want to improve your understanding of how they work and how

---

6

 Search Help - My Yahoo! Finance · Sport · News · Full Coverage · Weather

Search Result Found 3 categories, 199 sites, and 1 news story for world wide web guides.

You have just searched the whole of Yahoo!.
Try searching Yahoo! in the UK or Yahoo! in Ireland to narrow your results.

Category	Web Sites	Web Pages	News Stories

Yahoo! Category Matches (1 - 3 of 3)

Search Books

Business and Economy > Companies > Books > Shopping and Services > Booksellers > Reference > Titles > Writing > Research Paper and the World Wide Web, The: A Writer's Guide

amazon.co.uk
WORLD WIDE WE...
·Shop Online!
·8 books under £8!

Computers and Internet > Internet > World Wide Web > Information and Documentation > Beginner's Guides

Computers and Internet > Internet > World Wide Web > Page Creation > Beginner's Guides

Yahoo! UK & Ireland Site Matches (1 - 12 of 199)

Business and Economy > Companies > Books > Shopping and Services > Booksellers > Computers > Internet > Titles > World Wide Web

Regional > U.S. States > Massachusetts > Cities > Jamaica Plain > Travel and Transportation

- Jamaica Plain World Wide Web - dedicated to the residents of Jamaica Plain and to people wishing to gain more information on Boston and its surrounding area.

Computers and Internet > Internet > World Wide Web > Information and Documentation > Beginner's Guides

- World-Wide Web, Origins And Beyond - describes some of the historical aspects of the World-Wide Web development.
- Exploring the World-Wide Web - self-directed tutorial for new web users.
- All About the World Wide Web
- FAQ - World Wide Web
- ICYouSee Guide to the World Wide Web - a project of the Ithaca College Library designed to serve as a self-guided Web training page.

Computers and Internet > Internet > World Wide Web > Searching the Web > How to Search the Web

- How to Search the World Wide Web. A Tutorial and Guide for Beginners
- Research Paper and the World-Wide Web - companion site to the book. Features an online study guide with chapter-specific exercises.

Science > Computer Science > Courses > Courses Online

- Mastering Cyberspace: A Guide to the World Wide Web

Business and Economy > Companies > Books > Shopping and Services > Booksellers > Reference > Titles > Writing > Research Paper and the World Wide Web, The: A Writer's Guide

You can see that the number of categories is decreasing and you are starting to see links through to actual sites and pages. However, there is another sub-sub-category called 'Beginner's Guides' – we are in luck, it says there are 68 of them (in brackets next to the link). Click on it to go to screenshot 4. Here are a list of sites which (in theory at least) provide beginner's guides to the Internet. Click on 'All About the Internet' to visit a site created by a company called Imaginary Landscape – screenshot 5.

On the way through you should have noticed that categories and some categories within Yahoo! are always shown in bold. These are easily distinguished from actual websites and pages which are shown in plain text.

Searching Yahoo!

Having gone through the almost exhaustive process of working your way through the subject tree of Yahoo! with all its categories and sub-categories, etc you may wish there was a slightly easier way of finding information. There is. The Home page (and most other pages) gives you a search box. And perhaps the best way to learn how to use this facility is, again, by way of example.

Go back to Yahoo's home page either by clicking on the arrow to the right of your address box and selecting the correct URL, by selecting it from your history list, or by repeatedly hitting your 'back' button. Obviously if you have set this page as a default start page in your browser you have the option of clicking on the 'home' button. This time instead of clicking on the hyperlink 'Computers and Internet' go to the top of the page and type 'World Wide Web guides' into the search box. Then put your mouse over the top of the search button and click to initiate the engine. You will receive a screen similar to that shown in screenshot 6. The search has produced three categories with relevant information, 199 sites and one news story – a pretty satisfactory search.

If you look at the categories, you'll see that the second one listed:
Computers and Internet >
Internet > World Wide Web
> Information and Documentation
> Beginner's Guides
is the sub-sub-sub-category which we browsed through to in the above example. If you click on this link you will end up at

screenshot 4 – much more quickly than by browsing through the previous screens. However, since there are not those many categories listed, Yahoo! has been able to start listing the categories and the sites within those categories which include your keywords. Behold you can even see the site 'All About the World Wide Web' listed. So, by putting in a simple search you have saved yourself the time taken for four links and screen downloads.

Too Many, Too Few

In the search you have just performed (screenshot 6) Yahoo! had retrieved three subject categories and nearly 200 sites that matched your search parameters. If you had been searching for a broader subject, something as simple as 'Internet, 'computers', or even just 'World Wide Web', you could have retrieved tens of thousands of sites. Obviously there is no way that Yahoo! can display all of those on one page so it will limit the number of results that it will put on one page.

If you look down the list and do not find anything that you require you will get to the bottom and one of the hyperlinks that you find there will direct you to the 'next N matches'. In Screenshot 6, you can see that N is 17. Click on this link and Yahoo! will deliver up another N possible matches to your search phrase (17 in the above example). Again if you find nothing on this page at the bottom you will find another link labeled 'next N links', and you will also find 'previous N links' if you decide that you want to go back and have a look again. Yahoo! varies how many links are to be found on each page if not specified in the search terms, but N will usually be between 15 and 20 (20 being the standard default).

Now even if you are a sad person who loves sitting behind your computer screen looking for one minute piece of information you will not be able to look through 10,000 websites without going mad. In this situation you are going to have to refine your search to cut down on the number of sites. In other words you are going to need to control more closely how Yahoo! is searching its database.

Return to the Yahoo! home page and next to the search box you will see a link simply titled 'advanced search'. Click on this to find a screen shown below. These options give you certain parameters which will help you refine the data that Yahoo! finds in its database and deliver up more accurate listings.

Search by Date

When you start a search in Yahoo! the engine automatically assumes that you want to look at all of the sites that it has ever categorised. In Yahoo! terms this is over the last three years.

But on the options page you are able to select when the sites may have been added to the database. This is a way of cutting down on the amount of information that you receive back and makes sure that you are finding only the most up-to-date material on the Web. Click on the new listings box and you will see that Yahoo! gives you the option of looking at sites that have been added during the past three years (the default), six months, three months, one month, one week, three days, and one day.

Boolean Searches

Using Boolean operators you can get Yahoo! to retrieve any item that contains ALL of the words that you have typed or ANY of the words that you have typed. If you would like it to find sites that only contain all of the words then click on the 'matches on all words (AND)'. Should you want it to retrieve sites with any of the words that you have typed then click on the words 'matches on any word (OR)'.

Exact Phrase

If you were to go to the Yahoo! search engine and enter the word "bad" into the search, the engine would retrieve pages which not only contain information on "bad" but also those on "badgers", pages relating to "badminton", and you may even come across some sites dedicated to "badges".

If you click on "exact phrase match" Yahoo! will only find and deliver sites with exactly what you type. So searching on "bad" will retrieve sites with the word "bad" in their title.

Phrase

You can search on a phrase with as many words as you like simply by putting quotation marks at either end of the phrase or clicking the 'exact phrase match' radio button. For example, if you are looking for Neil Armstrong's speech you may put "One small step for man".

Search Area

Another useful way of limiting the amount of results that Yahoo! gives you is by telling it exactly where to look. In the options box you can ask it to:

- Search the whole of the Yahoo! database.
- Look for Yahoo! categories only
- Search only websites
- Look in Usenet groups
- Or only search e-mail addresses

And if you have already done a bit of browsing within Yahoo! you will find search boxes which allow you to search the whole of the Yahoo! database or only within the category or sub-category you are currently residing.

On the rare occasion that Yahoo! retrieves too few sites and/or categories you can try to increase the number of hits by lifting any restrictions that you may have placed on it. Try not limiting the date so that the engine searches the entire database that it has built up since it was created. Use the "OR" Boolean Operator so that it retrieves the site even if it only uses one of the words that you have typed in. Also try using wild cards such as the "*" symbol to allow Yahoo! a greater selection to choose from.

Other Directories

There are several other directory based search engines that you might like to consider.

Magellan

Not surprisingly all these other directories work in a similar manner to Yahoo! Magellan can be found at: **www.mckinley.com** The main difference here is that the Magellan indices give each site a rating out of 100% in how closely the engine thinks the site matches your search string. The 100% sites are the best (in Magellan's view) and these will be displayed first when you make a search.

Another useful feature of the Magellan directory, particularly for parents, is its use of 'green light' sites which have been passed as safe for children to visit. It is possible to search the database and ask that it returns green light sites only. So, if you are worried what children are finding on the Web, it may be worth setting Magellan up as your starting page.

Excite

This engine can be found at: **www.excite.co.uk** and has a look and feel fairly similar to Magellan, which is not surprising as they are owned by the same company! Like Yahoo! and Magellan you can browse and search but the reviews are fairly limited.

Go.com

This search engine can be found at: **www.go.com** and it is a directory as well as being a robot based search engine. It used to be known as Infoseek it can still be accessed through **www.infoseek.com**

Active Search Engines

When Web pages are being created at a rate faster than the staff of even Yahoo! can keep up there obviously has to be a better way of indexing all the pages on the World Wide Web. The only way that you can possibly hope to do this is through automation. So some clever heads got together and created spider programs. These spiders roam the Web looking for new URL's and reporting back to base with the details. It may be no exaggeration that one of these programs claims it can index as many as five million new World Wide Web pages each and every hour.

The main difference between the spider based search engines is how they index their information. Obviously since nobody is giving details of the site to the search engine it has to have a way of finding out what the page is all about. This it does by looking at the information on the page itself and sorting it through various programs to decide under which categories the page should be indexed.

False Drops

With the Web robots returning so many pages back to the search engine the databases tend to be on the large side. There is a lot of good information, but there is also a lot of rubbish. So it should come as no surprise, that when you perform the search, you receive back some of the rubbish along with decent information.

But apart from rubbish you will also get decent information which simply is not about the subject that you are looking for. In other words these are pages that include the search string that you put into the engine but use it in a different context. These returns are known as "false drops ".

Here is an example. You spent a long night surfing the Web and fancy a coffee in the morning. But you are bored with the same old taste so you would like some ideas for an exotic new brand of coffee for your filter machine. So you trot along to Lycos, enter the word "coffee", and look through the search results. Sure you will find lots of details of different types of coffee and even mail order coffee houses that will send it straight to your door. But you will also find pages on:

- The Coffee Association of Canada;
- FAQ's on caffeine abuse;
- Software for the point-of-sale in coffee shops;
- Lots of pages on the Java programming language;
- Sit down coffee shops in Beanhampton, New York;
- How to join the Coffee Brewers Federation; and
- A newspage on coffee merchants selling a new deal!

The bigger the database the more false drops you will get.

Go.com
Found at:

www.go.com

This is one of the largest databases to be found on the Web. It is a combination of directory and spider based search engines and attempts to index everything that it finds. So no level of importance is given to the occurrence of words on a page, or the context in which they appear.

As a result you will get an awful lot of false drops. But you will also retrieve documents that only mention the words you are searching for as a side line. This can be good as well as bad; false drops take a long time to wade through but you will be sure to find something on even the most obscure of subjects. To get some indication of the size of the databases created by the spider programs we entered a search for the words "steep skiing" into each of them. Go.com returned one of the largest number of pages, with a massive 222,037!!

AltaVista

Found at:

www.altavista.com

This is another of the larger databases to be found on the Web. Just like Go.com, AltaVista indexes everything it finds on a page, but it makes no attempt to filter out repeats, old pages or false drops. No surprise then that our search for the words "steep skiing" returned 2,512,510 hits. Well, I suppose we did require some information on steep skiing and we certainly got it. But on the plus side the more relevant sites did seem to appear at the top of the list. What is more, the couple of lines of text put your search into context as it appears on the page so that you can scan through the list of hits fairly quickly. Like Go.com you should use AltaVista when you are looking for something fairly obscure and are having problems locating anything using the other search engines.

Lycos

Lycos can be found at:

www.lycos.co.uk

and differs from Go.com and AltaVista in that it does not index the full text of a page. Instead it tends to use only the "important" words in a document, which it believes to be the title, the headings, and around the first 20 lines of the text. It also takes note of hidden tags that Web page creators put in known as "Meta tags".

This technique is used as a simple way of measuring what the page is all about. Logic states that the creator of a Web page will try to get across their main information as early as possible and that the headings will give a good indication as to what the following text is all about. Our search for "steep skiing" produced a miserly 4,243 hits which was a fairly good choice and they were all high quality. An excellent result.

Perhaps one of the best parts of Lycos' retrievable system is the fact that it gives you the retrieval score along side the title of the page. This is a ranking out of 100% as to the confidence that Lycos puts on its results. So a score of 100% will indicate that Lycos thinks it is certain it has found information that you are looking for.

A retrieval score of 90% will indicate that it thinks it is highly likely you will want this information but there is also a chance that it is a false drop. Another neat feature appears right at the top of the list of retrieved hits. Just in case we hadn't got the information that we were requiring, Lycos gave us the option to find more results in these areas:

- Pictures about steep skiing
- Personal home pages about steep skiing
- Books about steep skiing
- Reviews about steep skiing
- and a Yellow Pages of steep skiing, whatever that may be. (Perhaps I should give it a try next time and see if there is a company near by offering steep skiing!)

HotBot
Another huge database to be found at:
www.hotbot.com
which uses a different relevance scoring system to Lycos.

Our search for steep skiing produced 4,940 results similarly ranked with a percentage relevance score.

WebCrawler
This is supposed to be a slightly smaller database than the rest and can be found at:
www.webcrawler.com
However it still returned 10,658 hits for steep skiing and is a personal favourite.

Excite
Yet another large database which can be found at:
www.excite.co.uk
which provides some information for the Magellan directory.

Expanding Your Search
Just as with a directory search you can get more or less hits by:
- Using Boolean operators such as AND, OR and NOT.
- Searching for complete phrases.
- Using wildcard characters.

Metacrawlers

If you want to take a scatter gun approach to your Web searching pop along to:

www.metacrawler.com

for a search engine which does not even have its own database. This engine lives off the others and when you enter a search string it consults databases of the other leading search engines, which have already been mentioned, and then generates a retrievable list in its own format.

More Information

As you can see using search engines is more complex than it may appear on the surface. The quality and amount of information that you receive is highly dependent on the search string that you enter into the engine, and the choice of engine in the first place.

If you would like to learn more about search engines and how to get the best out of them then I can recommend "*The Net-Works Guide to Searching the Internet*" by Mark Neely.

Chapter 8

Shopping in Cyberspace

For anybody who is not heavily into shopping, the World Wide Web is a total boon. And even for those who have problems hanging onto their money, and just love to shop-till-they-drop, the Web is an absolute wonderland.

Just about everything new which comes along is condemned by old stick-in-the-muds as something which will "never catch on". And, just as before, they have been proved totally wrong. Perhaps it was said by traditional shop owners as much in hope as anything else but here are a number of reasons why shopping on the World Wide Web has caught on and why it is set to be one of the faster growing arenas of human activity this century.

Why?
Okay so you can buy books, compact discs, computer equipment, clothes, airline tickets, cars, underwear, holidays, food, etc., etc., on the Web, but why should anybody actually do it? Here's why:

Saving time
When you shop on the World Wide Web you are not limited to how far you can walk around the shops in your lunchtime or how long it takes to drive to the nearest town in your car. Nor do you have to turn up at the shops when it suits them between the hours of 9 till 5, or 4pm at weekends! On the Web your keyboard can do the walking and you can compare the prices between different outlets within seconds. It is simply far more convenient to sit in front of your computer, when you want, than to traipse all around the shops and still not find what you want.

Selection
The Web is particularly well suited to products which come in a large number of varieties. For example, books, videos and CDs. There are almost 100,000 new books published in the UK every

year so even if you could find a shop which stocks all of them, it would take you forever to find the one that you want. But the Web offers a perfect solution, as you do not have to look at the physical book itself. Instead you can simply enter a search string and have your computer produce a list of books on the topic that you are searching for. Better still, as you will see later in this chapter, you can get reviews on the books from your fellow surfers and compare it to all other available titles with the same information.

As for selection. When did you last shop in New York, or Tokyo? Shopping on the net lets you visit the stores of the world, and you'll never run the risk of being blown up by some terrorist action.

It costs less
Going into town to go shopping can be a costly affair. First of all you have the petrol for your car to consider which is a direct cost, plus parking, but you also have to fork out for lunch and perhaps a coffee just to keep you sane. Then you have got savings on shoe leather to consider not to mention the cost of the tranquilisers that you will need when you get home.

Discounts
Shops on the World Wide Web have far fewer overheads and do not need to employ half as many staff. They do not need expensive floor space on High Streets and they do not need to heat the building to keep you comfortable.

Therefore they can afford to sell the products much cheaper than a standard high street shop. As a result the World Wide Web offers a huge amount of discounts over standard products that you can find in your local town. What-is-more the immediacy of the Internet enables you to search harder for a better price for the same product amongst the different sets of retailers than it is on the high street. How often have you bought something only to find it cheaper four shops along. The searchability of the Web combined with the time savings should ensure that you always come up with the best deal.

It's nicer
Unless you are in need of serious help you can't possibly enjoy going out in freezing rain on a cold dark night after work (why is it that shops are open from 9-5 when most people work the same hours?).

Then who likes pushing through all those noisy crowds, fighting for some personal space inside a shop, and emerging into the traffic fumes of a congested city. By the time you get home you are normally, dirty, wet, and tired - rather like a drowned rat!

Why Not?

Given all of the above you might be tempted to think why you would ever want to go shopping on the High Street again. But here are a couple of reasons why not to "shop the Web":

Security

Perhaps it is because of the media, but a lot of people have concerns over the security of payments on-line. Without a doubt it is possible to intercept your credit card details when you transmit them from your computer to a server as you place an order. Secure servers have all but eradicated this and there is more information later in the chapter.

Delivery time & Charge

A lot of on-line sites such as the worlds biggest in amazon.com make a big deal about how quick they dispatch your goods. Despite having more than two million titles to choose from, amazon.com say they will dispatch your books within 1-2 days.

On the surface of it this looks like an extremely good service. But what you fail to think about at the time is how long it will take for the goods to reach you. Sure amazon.com may put them in the mail within two days but you still have to wait for the postal system to get the goods to your door. Secondly, you have to pay delivery charges, which may be calculated as a percentage of your total order, as a flat fee or based on the number of items you have requested. Using amazon.com as an example again, the books may be discounted by 50% but you will find yourself paying £2.95 for delivery of a single book. That's expensive! But then compare it to the parking fee of a city centre car-park.

Security

Let's get one thing straight. The World Wide Web is NOT full of vagabonds out to fleece the whole of mankind from the fruits of their labour. The whole issue of security on the World Wide Web is largely a media-led concern. As is the way in this country anything the media does not fully understand they like to sensationalise as a way of selling more newspapers and magazines. Just as we have not all died from flesh eating viruses (another favourite media scare story) so those who shop regularly on the Web have not had their bank accounts cleared out, their personal details altered, or their granny's maiden name changed by forged Deed Poll.

You would think that somewhere along the line somebody has been ripped off on the World Wide Web on the basis that there is no smoke without fire. But it seems to be a case of an awful lot of smoke from a couple of glowing cinders. Have you, or do you know of anyone, who has actually lost money via the Web? Indeed, although you will have read acres of newsprint telling you about the danger, have you seen any specific details of anyone who has lost money? I haven't and I've been buying on the Internet since 1993 – a lifetime in terms of Cyberspace.

Two forces drive this difference between belief and actuality. Firstly, self-interested parties largely generate all the scare stories. What better way to sell your computer security software than to make everyone think they are going to be robbed? Secondly, the technical side of the Internet is beyond most people, and it is a natural human reaction to be afraid of something you don't understand. So when we are told something is dangerous, we will believe them until we know otherwise.

Perhaps the main resistance to buying things on the World Wide Web has always been the secure transmittal of data and, in particular, credit card details. Until recently it has been virtually impossible to guarantee that no one could intercept your credit card details when you are transmitting them from your computer to that of the retailer. The concern is that somebody in a far-flung city or town will intercept these details and go around spending your money before they can be detected.

However, it is extremely difficult to intercept information on the Web. Yes, it is possible, but how many people do you know with the technical expertise to place "packet sniffers" in the gateway outside a host server? Furthermore, you stand exactly the same amount of risk by giving your credit card details to a person in a shop, saying them over the telephone or sending them in the regular mail. This is because the majority of credit card fraud is actually perpetrated by the employees of companies who have legitimate access to your card details - in other words the company that you are sending the details to in the first place. Just think about it. When you buy something with your credit card in a shop anybody who is standing around could write down the numbers from your card along with the expiry date. They would also be able to see how you sign your signature and it would not be beyond the ability of man to find out your address.

Certainly the person working behind the till will have a permanent record of the credit card number, the expiry date, your signature and your home address (for the guarantee). And have you ever wondered what happens to the carbon slip that goes between the papers on the credit card slip? These are imprinted with your card details and they are usually simply thrown in the bin for anyone to pick up later. Buying something over the net usually requires a delivery address. It is a brazen thief who uses stolen credit details to have goods delivered to their home!

Nevertheless it is a concern of people so the 'minds that be' on the World Wide Web are making progress to making it safer to send your credit card details down the line.

Secure Connection
You can be sure that nobody can intercept your credit card details on the World Wide Web if you have established a "secure connection". This connection, between your browser and the computer you are interacting with, uses a secret, or scrambled, communication channel which prevents anybody intercepting the information whilst it is en-route. If you are using Microsoft Internet Explorer you know that you have established a secure connection by looking at the status bar along the bottom of the window. On the right hand side you will see a lock appear if you have accessed a secure site. When the lock is visible it is ok to send your information. With Netscape Navigator you can tell you have established a secure connection by the key icon. A complete key indicates a secure connection, whilst a broken key indicates it is no longer secure.

Certificates
When you go to a site on the Web that makes out that it is a shop, how do you know that it is what it says it is? It may look like an on-

line shop but it could quite easily be a site set up by a hacker who has directed your browser from the true intended site to their computer. You could then be happily sending your credit card details for goods and services which simply do not exist and the hacker walks away with all your details to do their dirty deeds. It also works in reverse. When you go into that shop, how do the shop owners know you really are who you say you are? You could have quite easily stolen somebody's credit card and be using it to shop on-line.

The answer being developed for the World Wide Web is known as "certificates". This is a form of identification card which is generated by an independent third party. Certificate capabilities are built into most of the latest browsers including Internet Explorer and Navigator but the system of certificates is still in its infancy.

You will be able to obtain certificates from agencies - perhaps they will be free, or maybe you will have to pay a small fee such as £10 - which will enable you to shop on the Web free of any worries. No doubt this is the way of the future but there are legal hurdles to be overcome first and a worldwide standard needs agreeing.

Encryption

This form of data transmittal is growing rapidly on the Web, and it is one which Net-Works use on their book site at www.net-works.co.uk. It works by taking your credit card details from your browser and using 128-bit encryption to turn your details into an indecipherable stream of numbers and letters. That data stream is then transmitted to the shopping site's server. At no time during the transmission and reception are your credit card details held as human readable text.

In the morning, or whenever the shop deals with your request, they download the file from the server to their PC. The data is still encrypted. Only when they have the file in a safe environment, physically away from anything connected to the WWW, are they able to decrypt the information and retrieve your details. On top of that, the software 'key' that is used to decipher your information is virtually unique. Indeed the coding is so difficult to track that several Governments have tried to ban its use because even national and international security forces such as the FBI and Scotland Yard are unable to crack them. When you are using a site, which utilises encryption, you may not get the key or lock icons on your browser. However, when you reach the secure part of the transaction – usually the few lines where you enter your credit card details, you should briefly notice a grey area on your screen that turns into a different form of box from the others you will have been filling in.

On-line Validation

As indicated above, the main risk with credit card details lies with the humans who are the intended recipients of the details, but who are also fraudulent. Bearing this in mind, but also in the interest of efficiency, on-line validation systems have been developed. So in the future, when you transmit your credit card details, these will go direct to a bank or third party where they will be validated by a computer.

Authorisation codes will then be transmitted to the retailer in order to allow them to collect your money. At no time will a human come in contact with your card details. This on-line validation, combined with the use of certificates, will make shopping on the World Wide Web far more secure, and even safer than shopping on the High Street.

Alternatives

If, after everything that has been said, you still have reservations about sending your credit card details over the World Wide Web then there are some very simple alternatives. Most shops will provide you with a phone number so that you can call through with your credit card details or there will also be a fax number where you can fax through your order.

To save time writing everything out why not print out the order form by hitting the print button on your browser and then completing it and faxing it through to the company? You could also use the same method for sending an order through the traditional mail system. One final possibility is for you to send your order by way of two separate e-mails. In the first e-mail you send your credit card number and part of your order and in the second e-mail you send the expiry date for your credit card and your address details. It would be extremely difficult for anybody to intercept both of these emails and match them up, but the person receiving them will find it much easier. The difficulty for the fraudulent hacker here is that packet sniffers are designed to search out text strings which may look like credit card details. Neither of your emails will have this appearance so they have a far lower chance of being intercepted.

Buying On-line

The biggest obstacle to buying something on-line is probably your own concerns over security. Assuming these can be fulfilled by secure connections or the use of certificates, then buying something is simplicity itself.

In the majority of shops you can look through their catalogues and departments to find products that you are interested in. Once you have spotted an item write down its reference number or remember what it is called and then go to the page which is the order form. This may come in one of two forms:

- An on-line form where you fill in boxes and then hit a submit button. In this case your information is then transmitted by way of a CGI script to the shop's computer.

- A traditional form which you download onto your computer and then send back to the shop either as an e-mail, a fax or through the traditional mail .

Larger shops sometimes offer you the use of an on-line shopping basket (usually called a shopping cart as most of the software is made in the USA). This is just like using a shopping trolley in a supermarket. When you see a product that you like then you click on a button which adds it to your virtual basket. When you reach the end of your browsing session you then take your basket to the 'checkout' where the total bill is added up, the delivery charges are added and your credit card details are requested.

Once you have handed over your details, by whatever method, the transaction is completed and you can look forward to the receipt of your goods. If you sent your order electronically a lot of shops will send you an electronic confirmation of your order, and many produce an instant receipt in your browser, which you can print out and keep. And if there should be a problem with your order, such as a manufacturer not sending them to the retailer in time, then you will receive details in your email.

Chapter 9

Downloading from the Internet

Playing music, watching videos and wandering around three-dimensional worlds with your browser may be good entertainment but the World Wide Web is far more useful than that. All over the Web you will find sites where you can easily download files and programs for running on your computer which have nothing to do with the browser.

Software such as utilities, games, virus checkers, patches for Windows, screensavers, spreadsheets, typing tutors, and much, much, more. Indeed, if it is possible to do something with your computer then you will find a program somewhere along the World Wide Web that you can download direct. These programs on the Web come in three forms:

Public Domain Programs
These can be copied freely and distributed without hindrance. They can even be modified and resold without the author's permission.

Freeware
This is software made available free of charge by the author but are still under copyright, and certain conditions may apply.

Shareware
This, again, is copyrighted software and you are free to evaluate it on your computer free of charge. But once the evaluation period is up, usually around a month, and you found the software to be useful then you should pay a registration fee to the author for continued use of the program.

There are probably around about half a million public domain, freeware and shareware programs available on the World Wide

Web if you search hard enough. And the good news, this time around, is that there is an accepted format for the compression of the files that you come across. These files are known as "zip files" (not to be confused with Iomega's Zip Drive).

These files all appear with an extension of *.zip or with an extension *.exe once you have downloaded them. There are, of course, other forms of file available on the World Wide Web most notably the *.sit files created for Macintoshs and *.z, *.gz and *.tar files for UNIX computers. However these are few and far between and around 95% will be zip files.

The even better news is that all of these files (including the Macintosh and UNIX files) can be decompressed using a single program. This program is itself shareware and is known as WinZip and is produced by Nico Mac Computing. Without a shadow of a doubt this utility is a "must have". Without it you will not be able to decompress files that you downloaded from the World Wide Web and so you won't be able to use the programs. Besides, you will find it an extremely useful utility outside of your World Wide Web life for compressing and archiving files on your own hard disk.

Compression

Program files are often very large in terms of bytes or Megabytes. So putting them on the Web and downloading them would not be very practicable. This is because even with a fast modem it would take a long time to download them and tie up your phone lines for long periods. However if these files are compressed into a 'zip file' they take up much less space and download far quicker.

Obviously the software which performs such compression has to be fairly clever to make the file smaller but, when asked, will restore it to its exact original format (computer programs are extremely pedantic and even a slight change in the code will cause the whole thing to fail). The way that WinZip and other compression programs work is by looking at the programs and spotting long, repeated information-lines in the programming code. Each of these regularly repeated sequences could then be replaced with an abbreviation. Then, when decompression is required, the original long sequence is substituted for the abbreviation.

WinZip works extremely efficiently and you will be amazed at how small it can make even the largest of files. And on top of this it allows you to "archive" files into the same zip file. So one comp-ressed file can contain many original files such as the program, a 'readme' file, special drivers, and a registration form. Indeed, if you find yourself downloading sophisticated programs - and it is possible to even download program suites such as Office 2000 - the zip file may contain hundreds of archive files. Other popular Internet file formats supported by WinZip include:

- TAR
- gzip
- UUencode
- XXencode
- BinHex
- MIME
- UnixCompress
- Microsoft *.cab
- *.arj, *.lzh and *.arc (via external programs).

Downloading

In this section you will kill two birds with one stone because you will see how you can use your browser to download files from the World Wide Web, and the example file downloaded will be the latest version of WinZip! Fire up your browser and connect to the

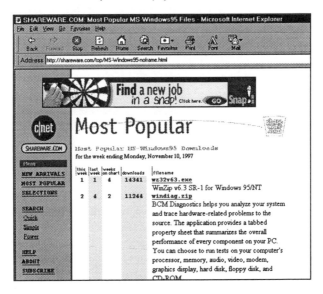

World Wide Web. Then, in the address box, type the following: http://shareware.com and hit return. This will take you to an excellent shareware site run by CINET. Here you will find the largest number of programs available on the Web and you will probably never need to look any further.

On the home page you will see that you are able to search its database of hundreds of thousands of programs or you can Browse through the files using the categories listed. You will also see three "special" categories for the most popular files downloaded from the site, the newest titles added to the site, and the top picks by the shareware.com team.

Probably the easiest way to get your WinZip utility is to click on "most popular" in the categories. WinZip is such an important utility that it almost always features in the most popular list. You will then be presented with a screen which looks similar to the one shown opposite.· When this screen shot was taken you will see that the latest version of WinZip is the most popular of the most popular files. This particular service release (an upgrade to take care of a small bug) has only been out for four weeks and has spent three of those in the number one slot. On the week in question no less than 14,341 Web surfers have downloaded the file to their computer. On the right of the statistics you will see the file name which is wz32v63.exe in this example. However you may need to look down the list of files and read the descriptions to find the latest version by the time you come to this site.

Once you have located the file click on the file name which will be a hyperlink to the download screen. Here you will be presented with a list of sites (computers) from where you can download the WinZip file. These are listed alphabetically

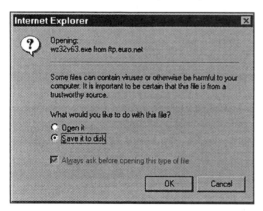

Before downloading a file, you'll be asked if you want to save it to your hard disk or open it immediately.

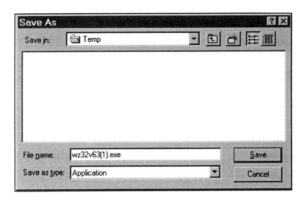

Save compressed programs into a temporary directory.

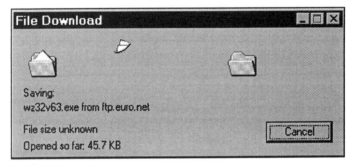

If the download is taking too long, cancel the transfer and try another site.

and include a reliability guide to give you some indication of how easy it is to connect to the site without any problems. The best strategy here is to try and pick a site not necessarily closest to you but one which will be quiet when you want to download the file. If you are trying to download the file in the morning then perhaps the best sites to go to are in the USA when most people will be asleep whereas if you are in the afternoon and the Americans are awake then you are better downloading from somewhere like Australia. Click on the file name at a site that you think is suitable. Your browser will then open a window informing you of the file you are about to download and from which site. There will probably be a warning that files downloaded from the World Wide Web could contain viruses. The shareware.com site will fall into the trustworthy source category but if you are still wary then you can check the file for potential viruses once you have downloaded it. You will also be asked if you would like to save the file to disk or to open it immediately. This is down to personal preference but saving it to disk is usually the least confusing option to take. It is also the cheapest in terms of connection time.

Once you click on the "OK" button you will be prompted as to which folder you wish to put the file into. Select a temporary directory somewhere on your hard disk such as C:\temp or C:\windows\temp. Then click on "save". Your browser will then open another window indicating that the file is beginning to download and showing you how many bytes of information have been transferred. If you made a note of the file size from the download page at shareware.com you will be able to get an idea of how quick the downloading will be. If you follow the advice of connecting to a computer where the local population will be asleep you should not have any problems. But if the file transfer seems to be taking too long it could be a good strategy to hit the cancel button and then connect to a different site.

Installing WinZip

Close your browser and disconnect from the World Wide Web. Then go to the directory to which you have downloaded the compressed WinZip file. You will notice that this file has the *.exe extension and not the *.zip extension. This is just as well, as without WinZip you would not be able to read the zip file! The *.exe extension indicates that the file is a self extracting archive. This means it will probably be bigger than a zipped file but it contains within it the software needed to extract itself onto your computer. Either double click on the file or run it from the "Start" icon of Windows. Then follow the instructions that will appear on the screen.

During the set up you will be informed that WinZip is itself a shareware program and that you will be allowed to evaluate it for 30 days. After that you should register a copy of the program with Nico Mac, and the best way of doing this is to send your credit card details. Once registered you will be sent a registration number that you enter into the program and which removes the "reminder" screen from the WinZip startup sequence.

At the end of the setup WinZip will be installed on your computer and will have integrated itself with your Windows desk top. Try using My Computer or Windows Explorer to open a folder. Now click on any file using the right mouse button. You will see a new option has appeared in the top area of the window which allows you now to add the highlighted file to a zip file directly. Using WinZip to compress and decompress files on your computer is another story, instead this publication will only deal with it in connection with your browser. If you are using Microsoft Internet Explorer you will not need to do anything more. WinZip automatically configures Windows so that *.zip files are associated with the program. This means that WinZip will be started up when you double click on *.zip files or when your browser makes such a request. Netscape Navigator is a bit different since it is not fully integrated into the desk top. Instead click on the Options button of the browser followed by General Preferences. Within Preferences select the "helpers" tab and look down the "file type" list. Choose application/x-zip-compressed and in the "action area" click on the launch application radio button. Then use the Browse button to locate your WinZip executable file which you will normally find in c:\programfiles\winzip folder. Then finish the sequence by clicking on "open" and "OK".

Congratulations you can now use the "open it" option when downloading a file from the World Wide Web and/or can open zip files when you have finished your surfing session.

Top Shareware sites on the Net

Site	URL	Windows	Mac
Cool tool	www.cooltool.com	✔	✘
Dave Central	www.davecentral.com	✔	✔
Download.com	www.download.com	✘	✔
FilePile	filepile.com	✔	✔
Pass the Shareware	www.passtheshareware.com	✔	✔
Rocket	www.rocketdownload.com	✔	✘
Shareware central	www.q-d.com/swc.htm	✔	✘
Shareware.com	www.shareware.com	✔	✔
Slaughterhouse	www.slaughterhouse.com	✔	✔
SunSite	sunsite.doc.ic.ac.uk	✔	✔
32bit.com	www.32bit.com	✔	✘
Tucows	www.tucows.com	✔	✔
Ultimate Mac	www.flashpaper.com/umac	✘	✔
ZD Downloads	www.zdnet.co.uk/software/	✔	✔

Chapter 10

Viruses and the Net

Successfully downloading files from the Internet and installing them on your computer is one thing, but how do you know it is safe to do so? It could be that you have just unknowingly downloaded a file that contains a virus. Although this is highly unlikely the consequences are just too horrendous to take the risk.

A virus is a software program that attaches itself in secret to an existing program and then adds some extra instructions. These unwanted instructions then set about having their bit of "fun" by messing with your system. At their worst they can do some pretty nasty things such as format your entire hard disk, destroy all the data and programs you have so lovingly assembled, or send porn files to everyone in your email address book.

And at best they will simply sit on your system for a long time and sporadically throw up humorous or strange messages when you are least expecting them.

The majority, however, fit into the middle ground and attach certain types of program or scramble sections of your data. In addition to virus codes attaching themselves to programs you may be unlucky enough to come across a "Trojan horse". These are nasty little characters which mascarade as useful programs but, when run, will do untold damage to your computer.

Signs of a Cold

You can get some indications that your computer may be infected with a virus when:

- Your computer slows down inexplicably.
- Strange characters appear when you type anything.
- Random error messages appear unrelated to what you are doing.
- And files are not where you would expect them to be.

Scanning for a Virus

Fortunately there are many anti-virus programs readily available on the market. You can even download some pretty useful anti-virus programs from the shareware site discussed in the last chapter.

These programs check out all programs and/or files on your hard disk for signs of a virus. If they detect any you are alerted and given several solutions to the problem. The most common give you the option to erase the infected file completely, for it to fix the problem, or for it to be removed to a floppy disk.

The problem with these programs is that they need a database of existing viruses to function properly. If you have been unlucky enough to download a file with the latest virus your anti-virus program may not know what it is, so it could reside on your system totally undetected by the anti-virus program and leave you unknowingly spreading the virus to everyone you share information with. The top anti-virus programs, however, partially get around this problem by allowing you to download the latest virus patterns from their Web sites. This updates your anti-virus database with the imprints of all the latest nasties that have been discovered.

Other forms of anti-virus program run on your computer and continuously monitor for any spurious activity. If they detect anything strange going on such as files being deleted or activities in parts of

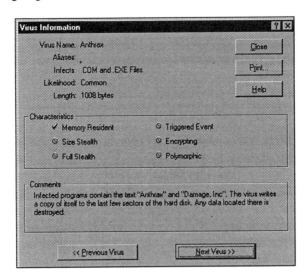

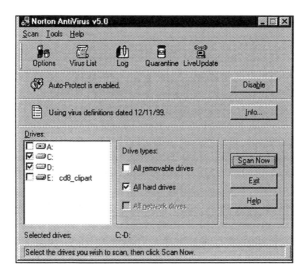

the computer that would not be expected, you are alerted. A program which can be recommended, and which will both scan your system for existing viruses and monitor activity around your system, is Norton Anti-Virus. Norton AntiVirus let you download the latest virus signatures from their website via their live-update feature. If you come across an infected file it gives you options to attempt to remove the virus, to put it into 'quarantine' till you have time to deal with it, or to safely delete the infected file.

Don't Panic!

It is not worth worrying unduly about catching a virus from the Web. The first thing to realise is that only executable files can carry a virus. This means that graphic files are completely safe to download because they are simple data files. Similarly text files cannot carry a virus. Nor can e-mail (but attached executables can). That should account for 98% of the stuff you will receive from the Web.

One set of viruses that appear, on the surface of it, to be an exception to the rule infect Microsoft Word document files and Microsoft Excel spread sheets. Viruses are contained in these documents as macros (a series of commands used within a program such as Word to accomplish repetitive tasks). Anti-virus programs are capable of detecting even these viruses before they can execute themselves.

Chapter 11

Bad Stuff on the Net

It is more than likely that you will have read or heard about the amount of bad stuff that is available on the Internet. Newspapers and documentaries claim that the Web is crawling with pornographic sites and paedophiles at every corner. Nobody, they say, is safe - least of all the children.

There have been reports of school children being abducted after making appointments to meet somebody they have met via the Web. And other reports of students making bombs at home using instructions they have gained from highly descriptive Web sites.

As a result, debate has raged over the validity of allowing dangerous material onto the Web. Should Internet Service Providers prevent such sites going onto the Web? Or should the authorities take a controlling hand? And then, what about the freedom of speech? The latter being a particularly strong argument over the pond where freedom of information is a cornerstone of the American Constitution. The World Wide Web is an information resource, they argue, and on-line censorship would be akin to book burning by an out-of-control dictator.

However it would be a fallacy to deny that there is undesirable material out there on the World Wide Web.

How Many?

Don't ever forget that the media like to sensationalise stories in order to keep you watching and make a name for a producer, or to sell more newspapers off the back of the story. But even bearing that in mind, how many Web sites, in terms of a percentage, do you think are dedicated to sex? And what about the more dangerous news groups. What percentage of those are devoted to sex?

What did you guess? Chances are that you would have gone for something like 10-20% or if you are a pessimist 20-30%. But you may be surprised to learn that less than 1% of news groups are devoted to sex and less than 0.5% of World Wide Web pages are deemed pornographic. Now, by way of a learning exercise, pop down to your local newsagents or garage and calculate the number of pornographic magazines on display as a percentage of the total number! So it follows that you are highly unlikely to accidentally stumble across undesirable material on the World Wide Web and this applies regardless of age.

But perhaps the main problem is something which few experts will admit to. Today's generation of children are the most advance in terms of computer technology that there have ever been. And they are an inquisitive bunch. No matter how well you hide material that you do not want them to see, they will find it. The deeper you put it the deeper they will dig.

There is also an argument to say that children exposed to the World Wide Web will gain first hand information in areas which adults may consider to be objectionable such as sex, drugs and gambling. This could help them mature faster and to learn for themselves instead of putting up barriers to the morals being pushed at them by over-protective adults. After all, for every Web site which advocates the taking of drugs you will find perhaps 50 which tell you how bad it is.

Stopping the Rot

Even so, if you are still concerned about the material that is available on the World Wide Web there is a whole range of software products joining the market which can be used to limit access to such information.

They all work in a similar manner by monitoring the activity of all Internet related programs (not just World Wide Web browsers) for certain key words and phrases. They function at bit-stream level which means that they monitor the data coming in and out of your computer (via the modem) instead of in the program itself.

This means that children can use any program that they wish, such as a Browser they may have brought home from school, and they still won't be able to bypass the controls. At the core of these monitoring programs is a list of addresses which may contain material that you wish to prohibit. These addresses are categorised into subjects such as:

- nudity
- drugs

- racism
- extremist organisations
- gambling
- cults

You are then able to limit access to all of these sites or manually override controls for the sites that you may think of as acceptable. Since new sites are coming on-line all the time these databases need to be kept up-to-date and you can usually obtain new files direct from the Web.

Perhaps the most useful function of these programs is to control the information that can be uploaded on to the Web in the first place. These prevent kids from providing personal information about themselves which could be of use to perverts and about your household which could be of use to thieves.

Some programs also allow you to limit the amount of time that your children may spend surfing the World Wide Web. First of all they allow you to set the hours that may be spent browsing the Web to a certain number per day or per week, and they will only allow access at a certain time of the day so you can stop them sneaking down stairs at the dead of night for a sly surf!

The Future

Faced with the threat of government intervention and legal restrictions many organisations are taking it onto their own back to do something about objectionable material. On-line organisations such as CompuServe and AOL have created kids only services which only contain material of educational or entertainment value. Other sites clearly label what is considered to be children friendly material. This includes search engines such as Magellan, discussed earlier, which mark such sites with a "green light".

Access providers and software companies are also working together in an effort to develop software programming and website standards that will allow browsers to detect when they are connecting to an adult material site. The popular RSAC system, for example, uses meta-tags to grade the level of nudity, sex and violence that is present on a site. These standards are proving difficult to lay down, however. The main stumbling block seems to be in coming up with an international rating system that would be acceptable in different countries with a multitude of different cultures. Consultations are still going on between software companies and market research companies, but a global solution will be probably impossible to find.

Age Verification

Age verification is the industry's attempt at cleaning up its image. Unfortunately, although its roots were probably well intended, it has been abused by many adult material sites.

The underlying principle is that you have to be at least 18 years of age in order to obtain a credit card. So, if you can enter credit card details onto a website with a valid number, expiry date and address then that should be sufficient proof that you are old enough to view the material. Nice idea, but there are a number of issues surrounding its implementation:

Firstly, there is absolutely nothing to stop Junior obtaining their parent's credit card and giving valid data which will give them access to the website. Of course, wrath will be poured down on the minor when their parents discover an unauthorised debit on their card but then the damage has been done.

Unscrupulous sites ask you to enter the credit card details as proof of age and then give a free period of access in return. Once they have the card's details they then start debiting it for monthly subscriptions until you go through the often-lengthy cancellation procedure. This obviously has nothing to do with age verification but is just a way of getting your credit card details in order to be able to bill you.

Age verification systems (AVS) have been set up where you trot along and obtain an actual certification, user name and/or password by using the credit card. Again this isn't so much as verifying your age as a method of getting money out of the card without overtly charging you for access to the site. It is a case of billing by the back door. You also won't be surprised to find that the web masters of the adult site receive up to $50 for everybody who signs up to the AVS system through their site links.

Protection Programs

Net Nanny, Cybersitter and SurfWatch are the three main child protection programs available for the Internet. You can purchase them via mail order or download them from the Web. Once installed, you update the underlying database by visiting the sites, and downloading the latest data via FTP.

Net Nanny
www.netnanny.com

Net Nanny has other convenient functions - tell Net Nanny what you do not want entered or received on your terminal. Select the terminal action you want to take for violations: Log the hit, mask words on screen, give a warning, block access, or shutdown the application.

SurfWatch
www1.surfwatch.com

SurfWatch tracks over 100,000 uniquely identified sites in the six core categories mentioned previously. Combined with dynamic pattern blocking, SurfWatch blocks access to millions of URLs, 5000 newsgroups, and 200 Internet Relay Chat channels that contain explicit material. Over 400 new sites are added to the database every day.

Cybersitter
www.cybersitter.com

Working secretly in the background, Cybersitter analyses all Internet activity. Whenever it detects activity the parent has elected to restrict, it takes over and blocks the activity before it takes place. If desired, Cybersitter will maintain a complete history of all Internet activity, including attempts to access blocked material.

Chapter 12

Building Your Own Page

Sooner or later you are not going to be satisfied with simply surfing the World Wide Web. You are going to want to make your own contribution and publish your own home page. For some people it will come as a surprise that anyone can put a page on the World Wide Web, without having to be a company or well known organisation. But the truth is that anybody with access to the World Wide Web can publish their own site.

There are pluses and minuses to this. On the plus side it means that everybody can have their say and anybody who is interested wherever they are in the world can listen. On the down side it means that an awful lot of complete rubbish is published on the Web making the decent stuff harder to find and slowing down the overall performance of the Internet.

To successfully publish your own page on the Web you need:

- Something to say; the easy bit.
- The page itself written in HTML (see below), and
- Somewhere to put your new page.

Saying Something

You really can put anything that you really like onto the World Wide Web. From a picture of you and your dog and a description of what you like to have for breakfast right through to an in-depth thesis on the space-time continuum and unification theory. But apart from complete vanity you can use it to help look for a job by publishing your CV, assist in the publicity for a cause you believe deeply in, provide valuable information free of charge to fellow surfers, or to sell something. In fact it is your imagination that provides the limiting factor. The only thing that you should look out for are pushing back the boundaries of decency. Even if your morals don't prevent you publishing material that may upset others, your ISP (or whoever you use to store your page) may see it differently. As discussed in the previous chapter the Web is rapidly moving towards the self regulation system and you could soon find yourself excluded.

You also need to make sure that you are not breaking any laws; not only of this land but also in other countries around the world - remember the World Wide Web truly is a global network. What is more you may find some restrictions placed on you by your Web provider. For example most ISPs will not allow you to use free space for commercial activity.

Creating Your Page

This is where it starts to get a little more difficult - but not as hard as you think. Any page that goes onto the World Wide Web needs to be written in HTML an acronym for a Hypertext Mark-Up Language. This is are essentially ASCII text with codes embedded for formatting things like text styles, paragraphs, tables and hyperlinks.

There are almost as many Web page editing programs as there are browsers. Some of these can be best described as a hindrance as opposed to an aid, but to others they are absolutely outstanding. Two of the best are HotMetal Pro from SoftQuad and Adobe's PageMill. These programs give you the options of creating your page in raw HTML code, just viewing it in "tags" and WYSIWYG (what you see is what you get). Using these packages it is almost possible to create a page simply by dragging and dropping elements onto the page and typing in the body text yourself. However, an understanding of how HTML works will make the job so much easier and speed the whole process up no end.

Understanding HTML is not hard at all, certainly when compared to normal computer programming. But it is extremely boring and repetitious. It essentially comes down to writing the page that you wish to publish using normal plain text then adding some tags which format the text you have already written, inserting a code of instructions for any images you wish to use, and embedding those all-important hyperlinks to further World Wide Web pages. It would take a complete book in itself to give you all the tricks of the trade concerning HTML. Net-Works publish such a book in Create Your Own Web Site. But you can find a decent on-line guide at the following address:

www.stars.com/Authoring/HTML/

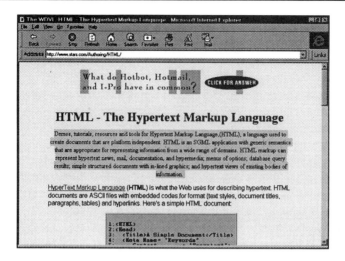

Getting Started

The quickest way to get a page off the ground is to turn to your trusted word processing package. Any will do, including the Windows Notepad. Now type in any line of text that you like, but for this example we will use the string "This is my first Web page". Now save this page onto your hard disk as mypage.htm and exit.

Having done that, fire up your Web browser, but instead of connecting to the WWW go to the file command and select "open" then use the "browse" button to locate the file you have just created. Click "OK" and you should find that your browser displays the text that you have just typed in. Congratulations this is your first page of HTML and it could go up on to the World Wide Web already if you should so wish!

Tags

Whilst there remains the option of simply putting up lines of text like you have already made it really would not be all that enticing or easy-to-read, and you would not get many return visitors.

To start adding a bit more visual impact you will need to use "tags". These tags tell browsers how to display the text that you typed into your page. They usually come in pairs; One at the beginning of the text and one at the end. And every time you want to change the look of a piece of text you need to end the tag style that you are using and start a new one.

Go back to your word processing package and open your file "mypage.htm". Now place your cursor in front of the word "first", and type:

<B>

then move the cursor to the end of the word "first" and type:

</B>

and save the page again.

Returning to your browser which should still be displaying your line of text, take your mouse up and click on the refresh button. And you should find that the word "first" is now displayed in bold. Go back, again, to your word processing package and this time place your cursor before the word "page" and type:

<I>

and move it to the end of the line and type:

</I>

and again save the document. Now using your Web browser click 'refresh' again and you'll find the word 'page' has turned to italics.

This time stay in your browser and go up to the 'view' command. Click on it and go down to the 'source' command. You should find that the Windows editor Notepad automatically opens in a new Window and displays your new page in HTML format. Use your

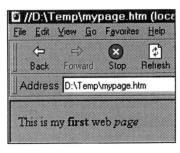

cursor to delete the italic tags that you have just inserted. Then close the Notepad Editor saving your changes. Press the 'refresh' button again and you will see that the italics have disappeared. You should be getting the idea by now. The tags are used to bracket the piece of text that you wish to format and always (well, nearly) come in pairs.

Headings

Return to the "view source" command from your browser and display your HTML code again. Place the cursor to the beginning of the text and enter two carriage returns. Now go to the top of the page and type "This is the heading". Return your cursor to the beginning and enter the tag:

<H1>

then to the end of the heading text that you have typed and insert:

</H1>

and save the file again. This time when you press the 'refresh' button you will see that 'This is a heading' is now displayed in large text.

Repeat the exercise but this time instead of inserting 'H1' inside the tags put 'H2'. Upon hitting the 'refresh' button you will see that the heading is still in larger text but this is slightly smaller than using 'H1'. Headings in basic HTML can actually come in six different sizes using H1 right through to H6; H1 is the largest and H6 is the smallest.

Structure

It is normal for Web pages to be structured in a similar manner. Although it isn't compulsory this is how the majority of documents are formatted:

<HTML> (this shows the document is created in HTML)

<HEAD><TITLE> (insert your title here) **</TITLE></HEAD>**

<BODY> (put your main text here) **</BODY>**

</HTML> (this is the end of the document)

You will see from this that Web pages have two parts, a header section and a body. The header contains the title and other information which is then displayed at the top of your browser window. Other parts, which won't be covered in this publication are used at the top or the header section to describe your page to search engines. The body of the page is that which appears in the main window of the browser.

Spaces and Returns

Standard HTML ignores all spaces, tabs and carriage returns in your text. No matter how many of these you insert in your document they will all be combined to produce just a single space in the browser. You can get around this for some browsers by enclosing your text with the tags **<PRE></PRE>** which means that it is pre-formatted text. However there are more conventional ways of doing things.

The single tag **<P>** is used to end a paragraph and create a single line break in the browser Window. The tag **
** will start your text on a new line. However two of these tags will create a line break and three will create two line breaks, etc. Don't worry about text wrapping because browsers perform this automatically and page width can be totally ignored.

Rules

A Horizontal line can be created using the **<HR>** tag and entering a few more details. In full:

<HR WIDTH=A% ALIGN=B SIZE=C>

where "A" represents the percentage of the page width that you would like the like to draw, "B" is its position using "Centre", "Left" or "Right" and "C" is its thickness. The default values using the simple <HR> tag is for 100%, centre and 1 (pixel).

Backgrounds

You can apply a colour to all of your body text by using the **<BODY>** tag. For example:

<BODY BGCOLOR="#008000">

changes the background colour to green. This code tells the browser which RGB combination it should use and you will find a list of the codes for different colours at the site:

www.stars.com/Authoring/Graphics/Colour

which contains enough colours to get you under way.

Images

Using images on World Wide Web pages requires a bit of an artistic insight. Nevertheless you might want to throw in one or two just for effect. The thing to remember is that the more images you have the longer it will take for your page to load. If it takes too long a casual browser will probably hit their stop button and disappear from your site, and that is the last you will ever see of them.

The smaller your images are, therefore, in terms of bytes and the fewer you use the quicker your page will load into a normal browser. So when you are creating your image to place on your page with your image editor make it as small as possible by decreasing the resolution. Also play around with format for your image to find out which creates the smallest image file for an acceptable resolution, is it *.gif or *.jpg? The easiest way of displaying an image on your page is to place it with an **<IMG>** tag or more specifically:

<IMG SRC="(image location)">

To show your image at its full size with adjacent text and bottom alignment. Extra specifications between the IMG and SRC will give you more control over the image:

<IMG   HEIGHT=200   WIDTH=300   ALIGN=TOP SRC="myimage.gif">

would display your image as 200 pixels high by 300 pixels wide and align it with the top of the highest item on the line. It is good practice to include an alternative to the image in text. This is for people who are browsing with the images switched off and will not know what its subject matter is. Again between the IMG and SRC insert:

ALT="(insert title of image here)"

and you won't get many complaints.

Links

This is probably the most important part of your page since the whole idea of the World Wide Web is to give documents another dimension by linking them to other pages. You do this by embedding links to redirect the browser to another address. This link could be by way of text, icon or an image. The text, icon or image will normally give some form of indication to the browser as to where the link will direct them but the URL itself is not normally displayed. Remember, however, that most browsers will display the address when the mouse is placed over the top of the hyperlink. To create a link to another page on the Web insert the following onto your page:

<A HREF="http://www.net-works.co.uk">Net-Works</A>

This will create a hyperlink from the name "Net-Works" on your page and direct the browser to the home page for "Net-Works". Why not try it out now with your browser? You may of course wish to create a link to another of your own pages. This means that you do not have to direct the browser to another domain, merely another page. You would enter something like:

<A HREF="books.htm">The Book Page </A>

This would direct the browser to the page books.htm within your domain. You can even embed a link within an image like so:

<A HREF="books.htm">
<IMGSRC="book.gif"></A>

In this case the picture of a book called book.gif is a link to the page books.htm. Somebody clicking on the picture of the book within their browser will be directed to your books page.

There are many other links that you can put in your page such as to newsgroups, telnet sessions and FTP servers. But perhaps the only other one that you need to know at this point is how to get mail sent to you. Do this with strings similar to:

<A HREF="mailto:sales@net-works.co.uk">Sales Department</A>

With most browsers clicking on the text "Sales Department" will open a "send mail" dialogue box already addressed to sales at net-works.co.uk

Inspiration from Others

Once you are happy that you understand the basics of HTML you can start to play around with your page and make it look a lot smarter. One of the simplest and quickest ways of enhancing the look of your page is to go for a surf yourself. Take a look around the Web and find some pages that you like then save these to your hard disk.

Once off-line, open these pages again using your browser. Then go to the command line and choose view source from the menu bar. Just as when you created your first page a Notepad will open and show you the HTML code behind the page you are looking at in the browser. From this you will be able to see how the Webmaster has created the page and what HTML codes he has used to get the effects.

You must be careful to stay within the bounds of copyright but it is not beyond the realms of possibility to cut and paste sections of the raw code from their page into your own. If you are only using small sections of the page there should be no problem but do not over do it. If you go too far you may find that the interaction between cyber-police and the uniformed variety is greater than you first thought.

Housing your Page

Now that you have created your first World Wide Web page you will need to find somewhere to put it. For most people the only option will be to put it on somebody else's system. This is because setting up your own server and connecting it directly to the Internet and all this entails would be prohibitively expensive.

For starters you will need quite a powerful computer, a top-of-the-range modem, a permanently open phone line, modifications to your computer to make it a "gateway", probably a router and a suite of server software. You will also need domain name software so that your computer can navigate the rest of the Web. All of this, and a little bit of consultancy to help you put it all together, could set you back by the better part of £5,000.

So, back to the cheapest way of getting your new page onto the World Wide Web. This is by leasing some space on your access provider's system on their hard disk. In return for hard cash they will set aside a certain amount of disk space for your sole use where you can place all of your files and where other Web users will come to have a look at your page.

Prices very considerably between access providers as to how much they will charge for a certain amount of disk space. Many are giving away free space with their Web access packages. But this isn't often much and is always laden with a lot of conditions. The main limitation for a normal user would be the fact that virtually no ISP's will allow you to use free space for commercial activities.

So if you want to sell anything or make your fortune on the World Wide Web you are going to have to look elsewhere. Expect to pay around about £5 per Meg for rented space. That should be sufficient for around 7-10 pages on the World Wide Web depending on how many graphics you use.

However there is ever increasing competition between Internet Access Providers and Web Space Providers which is constantly pushing down prices and so you should be able to find cheaper rates by shopping around.

The main advantage of putting your site on a provider's system is the speed of connection. Anybody coming to the site will be conn-ected at the same speed as if they were coming to your access provider's site. That is bound to impress other surfers since the speed of access is the major concern to users of the Web. What is more the company that houses your Web space will probably give you assistance in setting up file transfer protocol software which you will need for uploading your files onto their computer.

Chapter 13

Not Quite the WWW

As mentioned earlier, many people confuse the World Wide Web and the Internet. The truth is that the World Wide Web is just part of the Internet which is made up of a great many other facilities. This chapter will briefly mention some of the other aspects of the Internet, which you may find useful. You may already be familiar with some, but totally unaware of others. If you would like to know more about any individual part you will find further details in the Complete Beginners Guide to the Internet also published by Net-Works (please see page 128).

Email

Once you realise that email is short for electronic mail you can conclude that it does exactly what it says on the packet. You can send mail messages electronically between computers. This is probably the most popular resource on the Internet and it is certainly the most used. In the proper hands, and with a sensible approach, it can save you time and money.

The time savings are two fold. Firstly, it is much more immediate than traditional posting methods. Once you have written an email and clicked on the send button it will be transmitted to the recipient's In-box within minutes or at the most hours. Compare this to writing a letter which, even if you were to send it to someone a couple of miles away, would not arrive before the next day. But, perhaps the biggest savings are to be found when you are sending emails to people in other countries. A letter sent via airmail from the UK to the USA would take a minimum of five days to arrive whereas an email would normally take just five minutes. The second time saving can be found in actually writing, composing and physically dispatching your email messages. Typing on a computer screen is quicker than hand writing a letter and clicking the send button is streets ahead of putting a piece of paper in an envelope, sealing it, addressing the envelope, putting a stamp on it, and trudging down to the letterbox in the pouring rain.

Email Addresses

It may sound obvious but an email cannot be delivered unless you have the correct address. If you get a single letter or full stop in the wrong place your message will disappear into a void or at best you will get a "message undeliverable" note back in your own mailbox.

An email address is usually made up from a user-identifier followed by the @ symbol and the domain name of the computer (or disk space on a computer) to which your emails are sent.

The user identifier, for example, for Scott Western could be something like 'swestern'. And the domain name for sending email to me at Net-Works would be net-works.co.uk. So this fictional email address would be:

swestern@net-works.co.uk

Alternatives for this email account could be:

westerns@net-works.co.uk

or

scottw@net-works.co.uk

or

theman@net-works.co.uk

This last example shows that my user identifier does not have to be letters or initials from my name. It is simply how I wished to be identified on my emails. Some ISPs will allow you to do this (select your own user identifier) when you first set up your account, but others will impose an identifier created from your login name.

Sending an Email

If you think of sending an email in the same terms as sending an ordinary letter you won't go far wrong. First you need to enter the recipient's email address. Without this your email simply won't reach a destination. There are one or two on-line directories similar to a phone book where you can look up a person's email address, and there are smart programs which can search the net to find the address that you require. But by far the easiest way of finding somebody's email address is to call them up on the phone and to ask them for it!

Sending an Email

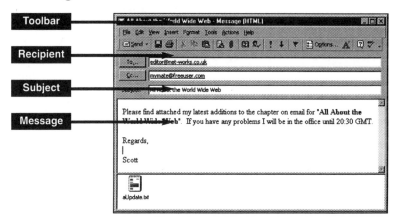

The next field is available for you to put in other people's email addresses who would like to receive a copy of the mail you are sending. The subject field is where you enter the subject of the letter. Many people tend to ignore this field as irrelevant and then wonder why their emails don't get read. If you put a good description in the subject field the person receiving the email will see that it is relevant and read it. If there is nothing there, or you simply put something like 'hello', they may leave it till later or in the worst case simply delete it without reading it (this is amazingly common amongst people who receive hundreds of emails every day).

The main body of the email should be like the text of your letter. Modern email packages such as Outlook, which works hand-in-hand with Internet Explorer, allow you to format the text that you are about to send. If you look at the example above you can see that "all about the World Wide Web" has been bolded and stands out from the rest of the message. Now you should note that the recipient will only see this formatting if their email package is set up in a similar manner, but it shows that emails are no longer a dull and lifeless way of communicating.

The final thing you will notice on the example above is that there is a file attached to the email. This file is able to reside anywhere on your computer and it will be sent along with the email whilst you are connected through your ISP. In Outlook simply click on the paperclip and then use the Explorer window to locate the file that you want to send. Click on the file followed by OK and it will be attached. The main purpose of attaching a file is usually to send a more detailed message from a word processing program or to exchange pictures such as photographs of holidays or of products for businesses.

Receiving an Email

When you receive an email you receive something like the screen shot above. In the form field you will be able to see the email address of the person who has sent the message and you will see your own email address shown in the 'To' field. Now you may query why you need to know the email address that it's been sent to since you have actually received the email.

This is because many people have several email addresses that are all forwarded to one mailbox. This helps them identify who the intended recipient of the email was and also gives them an insight into what the subject may be about. For example my editor has two email addresses, one which is **editor@net-works.co.uk** and the other which is **annsanty@net-works.co.uk**

If she sees a message to **editor@net-works.co.uk** she realises that it is most likely a business email from one of her authors. If she sees one to **annsanty@net-works.co.uk** then she realises that it is on a personal subject or from one of her close business

Receiving an Email

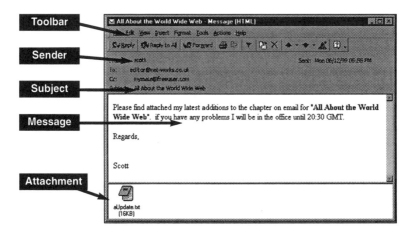

colleagues. The next field is a subject field which you already know helps identify the subject of your message when it arrives in the recipient's mail box. Directly below you can see the contents of the message and the fact that a file is attached.

Across the top of the screen you can see, and are probably familiar with, the buttons for dealing with this email. By clicking on the 'reply' button the email package will create a new message with the address and subject already filled in. This makes replying to an email message simplicity itself and explains why more emails are read and dealt with than traditional letters. The reply to 'all' button will send a response not only to the sender of the message but also to those who are copied in the cc field of the original. The 'forward' button will allow you to send the entire email that you have received onto a third party who may be interested in what you've just received. In the case of a simple 'reply' and 'reply to all' responses you are able to configure your email package to include the text of the message you are replying to or not depending on your requirements.

Email Etiquette

The problem with email is that it's a terribly non-personal way of communicating. You sit at your computer type some text onto a screen and then just hit the send button. Whilst this is a huge advantage over sending a normal letter you did not tend to feel so involved and therefore it is easier to write something that you may regret at a later date.

Don't forget that email messages are real even though they are usually transitory and in electronic format. A message can be copied, as you know, to lots of other people at a click of a button. It can also be stored on someone else's computer for a very long time. Finally, emails carry with them the weight of the law in just the same way as a normal letter. So if you Libel someone in an email you will face the same consequences as if you were to do it in a traditionally printed format.

Even if you are not breaking the law it is often difficult to portray your feelings when sending a message. Something that you intend to be a joke can easily be misinterpreted at the other end due to the lack of human signals. This has partly being remedied by the use of 'smilies' which are intended to tell the recipient in

Smilies

:-)	Happy smiley	The original and basic smiley. Means a humorous statement has been made, or a symbol of plain happiness!
:-(	Sad smiley	The opposite from the basic smiley. Means you are depressed about what you have just written.
:'-)	Crying smiley.	Indicates a really sad statement.
}:-(	Angry smiley.	What you are writing about makes you angry.
;-)	Winking smiley	Indicates a sarcastic comment or a flirtatious message. The reader shouldn't take your words too seriously.
:-o	Surprised	It is used to imply that the subject matter is surprising. Use a capital 'O' to indicate absolute shock.
:-\	Unsure	You are not certain what to make of it.
:-I	Indifferent	You are full of apathy and don't really care either way about the subject matter.
>:-)	Devil smiley	You are up to no good!
>;-)	Winking devil	You are being naughty, but it is all meant in humour.
8-)	Speccy smiley	You've got glasses or sunglasses on, or you are going on holiday.
:-p	Tongue smiley	You could be sticking your tongue out at the reader, or indicating that you are concentrating hard.
*<:-o)	Clown smiley	You are acting the clown, again.
~:@:	Piggy smiley	!

what sort of mode they have been sent. For example, a smiling face shows you may be joking, whereas a sad face will indicate you are serious and down hearted.

Usenet

Usenet is made up of a large network of news groups and the term often causes confusion amongst newcomers, with the Internet itself. On Usenet you will find more than 20,000 different news groups all dedicated to different subjects. These news groups are made up of like-minded people who have banded together to exchange their views on the topic of the news group.

Topics on Usenet range from the very serious to the extremely frivolous. You'll find highly scientific and political groups discussing complex subjects in fine detail and at the same time come across the named discussions centred around television soaps or third division football clubs. Whatever your interests, you are bound to find a news group that will cater for it and with more than 150 million people on the Internet you are bound to find some friends.

The software that you need to access Usenet usually comes as part of a package from your ISP. You will also receive a news reader courtesy of Microsoft if you have Internet Explorer on your system. These news readers will display and order (by date) all of the articles that have been posted to a particular newsgroup along with the name of the newsgroup itself. You are able to 'subscribe' to a news group and therefore partake in the discussion or to simply view the action from a distance. The same news reader will display more information about each of the postings such as the name or email address of the person who put the article on the notice board, the subject of the posting, the date it was received by the newsgroup and how big the message is.

When you have read a posting on a news group you are able to compose a message and reply to the group in the same way that you would reply to a particular email. You are also given the option to reply to the author if you don't want everybody else in the news group to read what you've got to say. Since it does look like an email it is easy to think you are in a one-on-one conversation but you must realise that news groups are totally different and you have a much wider audience – so be careful what you say! Also beware of other people's sensitivities; in the same way that you wouldn't walk up to a bunch of strangers and butt into their conversation, so you shouldn't stampede into an on-line discussion thread.

Anatomy of a Newsgroup Message

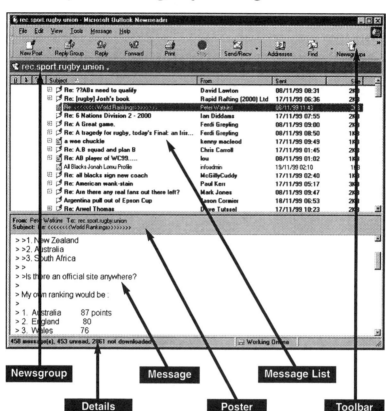

File Transfer Protocol

File Transfer Protocol (FTP) is the way in which you upload and download files over the Internet. It can be used both on the World Wide Web or through a direct connection to the computer which is housing the software you are trying to acquire. So, on some sites you would click on a link and have a file and a piece of software downloaded onto your computer via FTP. Or you may come across a link to a third party computer from which the file will be transferred. The later is most common on shareware sites. Most Web browsers these days will download files from the Web without you even knowing what's going on. And it's only if you are serious about file transfers, say if you're building a website for yourself, that you need to learn about special FTP software.

Internet Relay Chat

Internet Relay Chat (IRC) is very similar to Usenet but it operates in real time. So where you are viewing a message left on a bulletin board in a news group which could have been posted minutes, hours or even days before, with IRC you are only viewing messages and comments from other users as they are made.

IRC is a multi-user chat system that dates back to the 1980's (which is years before the WWW became popular). Even today it is considered as one of the most popular ways of communicating with other people on the Internet. Indeed, every day hundreds of thousands of people habitually log on to IRC to get their fix of chat. Yes, it's as bad as that; everyone agrees that once you get into chat you become addicted. Be careful this might happen to you, and you may lose all your real life friends.

Connecting to IRC

Just as with the World Wide Web, Usenet, and email you need a specific piece of software in order to access IRC. First of all you will need a 'client program' which usually isn't supplied by your ISP. The good news, however, is that IRC clients are readily available as freeware and/or shareware from loads of sites around the Web. To get your IRC client try popping along to: -

www.mirc.co.uk
www.megalith.co.uk,
or
www.nip.nl/mirc

where you'll be able to download the relevant programs along with extensive help files to get you familiar with the software and IRC in general. Once installed and fired up your IRC client will prompt you for the name of the server to which it should connect. Most clients will present you with a list which you can choose from. It is pretty much like connecting to your ISP and if you find you're on a slow machine try joining another.

Once you are connected you will find how easy it is to be welcomed into an IRC group. As a beginner it is probably best to choose any of the chat rooms (and you'll find many thousands of channels which you can access on topics ranging from aeronautics to zoo keeping and from full contact karate to Barbie doll collecting). Feel free to experiment with the various commands and to join in any of the discussions at any time as most rooms tend to be very friendly. You should also feel free to ask for help if you get stuck using IRC, but use a bit of sense and watch what is going on and see if you can work it out yourself before launching in.

Just as news groups display your messages to anyone who visits the news group and not just the individual you are writing to, anyone that is logged onto the same channel will be able to view what you are typing. Similarly you will be able to see what everyone else is saying on the same channel. This is true of everything that you say and type on your screen apart from commands.

Although you need to know some of the commands to use IRC you shouldn't be put off as they are very easy to learn and there aren't many of them. All of the commands start with a '/' and if you forget to put this in you will actually be speaking in the chat room. While this doesn't really matter, everyone who is on the same channel will notice and you'll get the same response as if you had broken wind at a dinner party. Some of the most common commands are:

/LIST   IRC is built up of many thousands of channels and rooms in which conversations are happening. So you can type the /LIST command to see which rooms and topics of conversation are currently taking place on the server.

/JOIN   Once you've got your list of channels and decided which topic of conversation you want to join in you use the /JOIN command followed by the name of the channel to join up.

/PART   When you are tired of the conversation and you want to leave the room all you do is type /PART which will take you out of the room but not out of IRC altogether (for that you need /QUIT).

Appendix A

A Brief History of the Net

Around 20 years ago the Cold War was at its peak. The USA and Soviet Union were at eachother's throats, armed to the teeth with highly destructive nuclear weapons. These missiles, of course, required computers to launch them and those computers had to be linked in a network to ensure a coordinated attack when the time came for all out war.

In those days not only were computers physically large in comparison to today's machines but the networks were extremely rigid, working to a strict hierarchical structure. Each machine could only communicate with the others in its network once it had asked permission from its 'chief' computer. That chief, conversant with the paranoia of its military controllers, would decide if the computer in question was allowed to talk to the others and how quickly the message would be passed on.

Whilst giving the military leaders more control, it was the use of this 'chief computer' which could have proven fatal in the case of a war. Just one well-placed Soviet attack would have been able to take out the chief and hence sever communications to the rest of the network. Appalled at such a prospect the military boffins banded together and introduced a new project. Called Advanced Research Projects Administration (ARPA) was given the brief to design a new set of computers that would be able to withstand a directed attack.

The result was ARPAnet - a military network which worked on the principal of 'unreliable computers'. In other words each computer in the network assumed that its counterpart was unreliable and prone to 'go down' at any point. The same computer was also charged with the task of making sure that its commands would be carried out. The only way to do this was for a map of computers to be created with each one given a personal address and location. These locations were then stored in a database and made available to every computer in the network.

So the need for a 'chief' computer was totally removed. By checking at regular intervals to see that its counterpart computers were still functioning, any individual computer could send a message to another either directly or around the network if it realised it was not getting any response.

Pivotal to the whole concept was TCP/IP (Transmission Control Protocol/Internet Protocol) Software. This software regulated how each of the computers would communicate with the others. In other words it made sure that each computer in the network was 'speaking' the same language and removed the need for 'translators'.

ARPAnet worked extremely well, but those in charge believed that there was room for improvement. So a small number of academic sites were allowed to join the network to study it and suggest amendments. Excited by the prospect of their new 'toy' the academics took it to their heart and requested that other sites be accessed by the same network. And it was not just academic sites that realised the benefits of such a network. Institutions around the world began to see the ARPAnet working environment as an attractive way to link up computers from whichever state or country, in a cheap and practical way.

And rather intriguingly, for a project which had its beginnings in the military, it was also seen as a very efficient and altruistic way of sharing information between all of these institutions.

It is from these small beginnings that the Internet has grown today. It is now a global communications port, linking computers and networks in institutions, businesses and even individual homes around the world.

Appendix B

Netiquette *and* how to be a good netizen!

I want to join

If you wish to be added to/removed from a mailing list contact the separate subscription address, not the list itself.

FAQ - Frequently Asked Questions

If you want to participate in a group, ask the moderator or search the associated Web pages for a list of FAQ's. This will bring you up to speed on the topics in the group and save you wasting yours, and others' time.

Check your address

Make sure you give your address correctly and always check you are sending your message to the correct person/group.

Follow the thread

Like in any conversation, you should listen in for a while before adding your bit. Before jumping into a mailing list discussion or a newsgroup read a few postings and then think about your reply first.

Be focused

Make sure you tailor your contribution to a Usenet group's main area - eg. a knitting circle is not interested in the latest bug fixes for Windows.

Make room

When you have finished surfing log out quickly. This will free up time for someone else. Make sure you follow the correct logout procedure rather than just unplugging your modem.

Keep to the point

Verbal diarrhoea can be painful; the same can be said when surfing. Keep your messages clear and concise, focus on one point, and make your title relevant for easy searching. Use acronyms sparingly having first used the long-winded version. Use hard returns at the end of lines or your recipient may have difficulty reading your message.

Shouting from the rooftops

Shouting when surfing is frowned upon, and ANYTHING IN CAPITALS IS CONSIDERED AS SHOUTING. If you need to emphasise a point try using icons, or asterisks.

Testing

You can test out your files by posting them to alt.test or misc.test. This way others do not have to look at your test files.

Be a team person

By joining in a group discussion you are becoming a team player. Address your discussion to the group, not an individual. Use Email for one-to-one chats. Ask for all replies to your question to be sent to you. Then read them and post a general reply back to the group.

Offensive

There are those who will be rude on the net. An offensive file is called a flame and you should not send them, or reply to them, but ignore them. You can set up a global kill file so that offensive words are not passed on to you.

Think before you speak

You know the problems of shooting off your mouth, so beware letting off steam from your keyboard. Think, before you speak, before you type! A message from you can be used by others for flaming, libel proceedings etc.

Tone

Some people come across as much more aggressive when they write than when they speak. You can make your messages friendlier by using accepted icons – see smilies.

Sorry

Learners on the road can drive you mad, but you were a learner once. The same can be said on the ski slopes and on the net. Forgive people once for netiquette blunders, but not twice. Show others how to be helpful and polite and it should be reciprocated.

Credit where due

If you reference anyone else's work, make sure you give it due credit. Emails and HTMLs are subject to the laws of the country for libel, breach of copyright, slander etc. So think before you slag anyone or anything off. Your Email may be taken down and used in evidence against you!

Privacy

The net is a global place but Email is private and meant for you. Just like you probably wouldn't photocopy a private letter and send it on, it's considered bad form to send on private Emails without first asking the author's permission.

Remind me

Some people send and receive hundreds of Emails every day. When replying put the gist of the original request in at the start so they know what you are referring to. An informative subject heading can be enough.

What time is it?

Make sure your computer's clock and date/time facilities are correct. This is appended to your message and used as reference by others.

Help!

You need to be able to help others to help you. If you have a problem make sure you know what to say when calling technical support. They will nearly always need you to verify who you are so have this important information easily to hand, along with the support teams' telephone number. Also you may need to be able to tell them your software serial number, customer reference number, the version of software you have etc before you get on to your specific problem.

Graphics

Use small graphics images in your html documents as you do not know the speed of a recipient's modem. If you use video or voice files give some idea of their size.

Sign off

Include your signature with all emails so that others can contact you.

Glossary

Access provider

May also be referred to as an ISP (Internet Service Provider). A company which will sell you an Internet connection. It will have installed its own FTP, Gopher, Archie, news, mail and Web servers and will provide you with the necessary software to use them.

Anonymous FTP

A way of logging in to a computer and downloading files by FTP without having to identify yourself (so you don't need TCP/IP). Usually you log in as Anonymous and use your Email address as the password.

Backbone

High speed data connections joining the big access providers. Smaller access providers need to connect to a backbone provider to gain access to the backbone. In WAN's it is the central section of the network.

Baud rate

Used mainly when referring modems. It is the speed at which data can travel along a channel, in terms of bits per second.

Binary

Computers work by counting in ones or zeros which is known as binary. Files stored on a computer may be either binary or ASCII. In a binary file the data is stored in seven-bit bytes; in an ASCII data is stored in eight-bit bytes. Most systems can read ASCII files but not all can read binary. Programs are usually binary, while Emails are more likely to be ASCII. Most Email packages do not allow the transfer of binary files.

Bits/Bytes

A bit is the smallest piece of information that a computer recognises and it's either got a value of zero or one. A byte is a group of either seven-bits or eight-bits.

Bps

Bits per second. The speed at which data can be transferred between pieces of hardware. You are most likely to come across it in relation to how fast modems work.

Browser

To download and read documents taken from the World Wide Web you need a software program called a browser. Most common are Netscape, Mosaic and Microsoft.

Client

Software on a computer which is used to request information from the Internet. When you call up a web page you are acting as the client, and the computer you have contacted is the 'server'.

Dialup

A non-permanent connection to the Internet. A dial-up account will not use TCP/IP, so you can not be recognised.

Domain name

An Internet identification name that specifies where your computer can be contacted. Written as a series of letters separated by full stops and slashes; for instance ours is net-works.co.uk

Download

The process of copying a file from one machine to another (usually yours).

Email address

An address which identifies you on the Internet and allows others to send you Email. There may be many people at a domain name, so the Email address can identify a particular person at a particular address. It is made up from your name, the symbol @ (pronounced at), and the domain name. e.g. sales@net-works.co.uk.

FAQ - Frequently Asked Questions

This is a document found in most Usenet groups. It will have questions (and answers) that are most commonly asked by newcomers to the group. Read it before you post any questions in a group.

Flame

A rude message usually posted to a group or person. Flames are considered offensive and those who do it find themselves shunned. A flame often incites retaliation with horrible consequences. Do not get involved in flame throwing.

Firewall

It will not protect you from flames, but it is a security measure preventing access to a LAN from outside networks, e.g. the Internet. Many companies do not want others to be able to access their LAN.

Gateway

A device which translates an incoming flow of data from an outside network so that it can be used on a LAN. A gateway can be shared by many users.

Gopher

Software that searches the Net to find information for you. You need a Gopher client on your machine - the host machine must have a Gopher server application. Most browsers now have a Gopher facility. Gopher is menu driven and it reads and downloads documents based on your criteria. These documents can then be read off-line.

Home page

It has two meanings. It is the first page of a company's web site and the one you will be taken to as default. Also generic term for the whole web site of a company or individual.

Host

Another computer on the Internet which allows users to connect to it. An ISP's computer is a host computer.

HTML - Hypertext mark-up language

You need to know this language to create docu-ments to go on the World Wide Web.

HTTP - Hypertext Transfer Protocol.

The way to transfer HTML documents between the client and the Web server (so others can then see them on the WWW).

Hypertext

Text on your screen which you click to take you to another document in the same web site or at another. Hypertext links form the basis of the World Wide Web. When creating a web site the author uses HTML to put up hypertext.

ISP

See Access Provider.

IP - Internet Protocol

This is a standard which devices on the Internet use to communicate with each other. It describes how data gets from its source to its destination.

IP address

Your Email address uniquely tells the Internet who you are. Computers need to know this but they prefer to deal in numbers so your address has a decimal notation known as your IP address.

IRC

Internet Relay Chat. An Internet resource allowing you to chat in real time to anyone else connected to the same chat room.

ISDN

Integrated Services Digital Network. It is a network which allows you to send information in a digital form over the existing telephone lines at speeds of 128Kb. You dial the computer you wish to access, establish a connection and send your information very quickly. ISDN lines can be installed by BT but they are more expensive to install and rent than a normal telephone line.

LAN

Local area network. A group of computers and peripherals connected to form a network where they can talk to each other. They can vary in size from just computers in an office to hundreds across several buildings.

Metasearch

A search engine that works by querying other search engines.

Modem

*MO*dulator *DEM*odulator. A device which can send and receive information. It either receives information from your computer, converts it into analogue signals, and then passes them down the telephone line to another computer. Or, it takes a signal from a telephone line and converts it into a form your computer can understand. Modems operate at different speeds.

Moderator

A person who checks all the mess-ages received by a newsgroup ensuring they are on topic. Cynics call them censors.

Newsgroup

Internet bulletin boards where you can find out everything there is to know. There are thousands for every subject imaginable and collectively they are known as Usenet.

Packet

Data that is bundled before sending across a network is called a packet. It has inform-ation such as where it is from, where it is going, what is in it and what form it is in so that the recipient computer can read it.

POP- Point of Presence

An access point set up by an Access Provider. There will be many around the country so that you can make a local priced call to a POP and then get on to the Internet.

PPP - Point to Point Protocol

It allows IP connections between two devices over both types of circuits. When you connect to your ISP you are probably using a PPP connection.

Protocol

A standard for how two devices communicate with each other, a common language.

Router

Connects together all the networks that make up the Internet and allows the transfer of packets.

Server

A central computer, often a dedicated PC, which makes data available to the Internet.

SLIP

Serial Line Internet Protocol. Now being superseded by PPP, it is a standard which allows devices to use IP over asynchronous and synchronous links.

Spam

Internet slang for when someone indiscriminately sends the same message to various newsgroups. No one appreciates it.

TCP

Transmission Control Protocol. The major standard of all the Internet Protocols. TCP makes sure packets get from one host to another and that what they contain is understood. It takes the data to be transmitted from the application and passes it onto the IP for transmission.

Unix

An operating system running on a host machine allowing many clients to access the host's information, at the same time. Used by many servers on the Internet.

Upload

When you send a file or message from a computer (usually yours) to another computer (usually the host) you have uploaded your data.

WAIS

Wide Area Information Server. Allows a client to do a keyword search on several online databases at the same time.

WWW

World Wide Web. Commonly known simply as 'The Web', it has opened up the Internet to world-wide use. All documents on the web are hypertext-based meaning they can all be linked together. You pass from one to the next by clicking on a particular word. Could soon become the definition of The Internet.

Zip File

A compressed file with the extension *.zip – don't confuse with a Zip drive.

The Net-Works Guide to
Creating a Website

The World Wide Web has established itself as an important business and communications tool. With hundreds of millions of computer users around the globe now relying on the Web as their primary source of information, entertainment and shopping, it cannot be ignored.

Whether it is to showcase your business and its products, or to present information on your favourite hobby or sport, creating your own Web site is an exciting development. But unless you're familiar with graphics programs and HTML (the "native language" of the Web), as well as how to upload files onto the Internet, creating your Web pages can also be very frustrating! But it doesn't have to be that way.

Web Publishing Made Easy

This book, written by a Website design and marketing consultant, will help demystify the process of creating and publishing a Web site. In it you will learn:

- How to research and plan your site,
- What free tools are available that make producing your own Web site child's play (and where to find them),
- How to create your own dazzling graphics, using a variety of cheap or free computer graphics programs,
- How to put it all together to achieve a great look with a minimum of fuss, and
- How to promote your Web site and attract other Internet users to it.

Advanced Web Design Issues

In addition to canvassing the basics of creating your first Web site, the author also discusses more advanced Web design issues... how to focus your Web site content for your target audience... how to minimise the time taken for your Web site to download... and what lies ahead for the Web and eCommerce... etc., etc.

Tim Ireland   112 pages   £6.95

The Net-Works Guide to
Marketing Your Website

Simply creating a website and putting it on the Internet is not enough to generate online sales, no matter how good it looks. In Cyberspace there simply isn't any passing traffic. The customer is king, and they will selectively choose which sites they are going to visit. Indeed, without a well thought-out and successfully implemented marketing plan, the majority of your potential customers will not even know that you are out there.

What is more, even if you have a few years of 'real life' marketing experience under your belt, you have a lot to learn, and unlearn, before attempting to market your website. The Internet is a very different medium from those you may be used to, and your marketing strategy will have to adapt accordingly if you want to enjoy any kind of success.

Online Marketing Made Easy

The Net-Works Guide to Marketing Your Website will show you how to construct and deliver a successful promotional strategy. It covers everything from the basics of linking to other sites and search engine registration, through to referral sales and associate programs. No stone is left unturned in the quest for more visitors. You will learn:

● How to promote your site in newsgroups and chat rooms without being flamed,
● The importance of META tags and how to use them,
● How to build customer loyalty,
● What is meant by 'sticky content' and how to write it,
● Why e-zines, newsletters and bait pages are important,
● Ways of promoting your site in the traditional media,

Anyone reading this book, and putting its easy-to-follow, non-technical advice into operation, can expect a rapid increase in the number of hits to their website.

Tim Ireland   112 pages   £7.95

Starting and Running a Business on the Internet

Do you want to:
- ✔ Sell your goods all over the world without leaving your office chair?
- ✔ Tap the fastest growing and most affluent market ever?
- ✔ Slash your marketing and advertising costs?
- ✔ Talk to the other side of the world for free?
- ✔ Have access to strategic information only the biggest companies could afford?

Then your business should be on the Internet!

Companies are already cutting costs, improving customer support and reaching hitherto untapped markets via the Internet. They have realised the potential for this exciting new commercial arena and they've grabbed the opportunity with both hands. Now you can join in the fun of what is still a 'ground floor' opportunity.

Starting and Running a Business on The Internet offers realistic and practical advice for any existing business or budding 'Cyberpreneur'. It also:

- ❑ Helps you get started QUICKLY and CHEAPLY.
- ❑ Tells you which sites 'work', which don't and, more importantly, WHY!
- ❑ Details how to PROMOTE your business online.
- ❑ Shows you how to stay ahead of your competitors.
- ❑ Warns you of the major PITFALLS and shows you how to AVOID them.
- ❑ Highlights important issues like CREDIT CARD handling and site SECURITY.

Alex Kiam   112 pages   £6.95

Book Ordering

To order any of these books, please order from our secure website at **www.net-works.co.uk** or complete the form below (or use a plain piece of paper) and send to:

Europe/Asia
TTL, PO Box 200, Harrogate HG1 2YR, England (or fax to 01423-526035, or email: sales@net-works.co.uk).

USA/Canada
Trafalgar Square, PO Box 257, Howe Hill Road, North Pomfret, Vermont 05053 (or fax to 802-457-1913, call toll free 800-423-4525, or email: tsquare@sover.net)

Postage and handling charge:
UK - £1 for first book, and 50p for each additional book
USA - $5 for first book, and $2 for each additional book (all shipments by UPS, please provide street address).
Elsewhere - £3 for first book, and £1.50 for each additional book via surface post (for airmail and courier rates, please fax or email for a price quote)

Book	Qty	Price
	Postage	
	Total:	

☐ I enclose payment for £_____

☐ Please debit my VISA/AMEX/MASTERCARD

Number: ☐☐☐☐ ☐☐☐☐ ☐☐☐☐ ☐☐☐☐

Expiry Date: ☐☐☐☐   Signature: Date:

Name: _____

Address: _____

_____

_____

Postcode/Zip:_____

Telephone/Email:_____

NGInternet